My Life Story

GH00738727

John G Acton

ISBN-13:
978-1530446520

ISBN-10:
153044652X

Published by Pianist Storyteller Novels in March 2016
(26 Holmwood Avenue, Shenfield, Brentwood, Essex,
CM15 8QS)

Details of his six children's and teenage novels can be
found on his Internet blog site :-

<http://pianist-storyteller.blogspot.com>

The novels and this autobiography are also available from
Amazon where he has been given an author's page using
the shorter version of his name, John Acton.

Short Summary of "My Life Story"

John G Acton was born in December 1920 in a London East End terrace house. At 95 with an OBE and LRAM (Piano), 68+ years of happy marriage to his talented wife of 93, five wonderful children (eldest son also an OBE plus) all with happy families, 8 grandchildren and 6 great-grandchildren to date, John has written for them this record of his life.

Part One "Very Earliest Memories."(1920-1932)

John describes his childhood, home and daily life in the Twenties and early Thirties in minute detail.

Part Two - "From Dancing Fingers to Talking Feet" (1932-1938) Piano studies compete with secondary school studies. . Culmination is taking part as one of 14 juvenile pianists in the 1937 film "Talking Feet" starring Hazel Ascot, a nine year old tap dancer, (currently shown at times on TV channel 81).

Part Three - "Epilogue" (1939-2015) A 40+years career in Customs and Excise was interrupted by five years war service as a Corporal Wireless Mechanic. Then marriage to Doreen Mason completely changed his life. They joined the Brentwood Baptist Church. John restarted the Christian union in Customs HQ and spent 38 years as a youth leader in the Brentwood Boys Crusader Class. Retirement from Customs at 60 allowed John to spend almost 30 years teaching piano at home and writing 6 novels for children and teenagers.

Acknowledgments and Dedication

As stated above my wife completely changed my life. Then I have sought her advice and sometimes her memory at every stage of this work. So 'My Life Story' is dedicated to her. I am also most grateful to my youngest son James, whose computer expertise has so often helped me out in my literary efforts. My family have generally given me encouragement. John G Acton, 26 Holmwood Avenue, Shenfield, Brentwood, Essex CM15 8QS – johngacton@gmail.com

PART ONE - Very earliest memories (1920-1932)

Mrs DAISY ACTON) (Nee BATES)

Chapter 1

I have heard that hypnotists can help your memories go back as far as your mother's womb. One of my daughters once asked me to record some soothing music to play to her baby while still awaiting birth.. My mother was a good pianist: Listening to her play was probably among my early memories.

But my own earliest memory was undoubtedly her beautiful face and soft voice. I loved her intensely. She was very talented in amusing me, cooking wonderful meals and in home dress-making. She taught me my ABC and how to spell my name and some simple two or three letter words. She also got me to say simple 'God bless........' prayers before going to sleep.

Coming back to my very earliest memories, I soon became aware of my Dad. His tall figure with a moustache and prickly kiss was so different from my Mum's soft touch. I saw little of him during the week as he commuted daily to his job in the central Custom House, Lower Thames Street, London. I remember he used to pause briefly before he left in the morning, smile and say, 'Have a really good play to-day John.'

John (myself) , Mum and Ken

Soon it was my four and a half years older brother Ken, who began to dominate my attention, as I crawled out of the 'bawling baby' stage. Once I had begun to speak a little more, we soon got talking and had great fun together, plus a little rivalry for Mum's attention. He used to tease me at times with improbable stories.

One of these started with the hero seeing a swarm of little aeroplanes emerging from a cave on the beach. He asked me to agree it was a good start for a story. So it was, but I could never get him to tell me what came next. I also remember one time when Mum was trying to get me to eat a little cheese. I resisted. Then Ken offered me a tempting morsel. I tried it and yelled. I was later told it was very strong 'Blue Vinny'.

As a toddler, I used to like walking under the kitchen table, (the actual one we use today, ninety years later). As I grew taller, I was close to bumping my head. My Mum told me to stop doing it, or I might get a nasty knock. Then she told me that if I hurt myself she would not comfort me. The inevitable happened: crying, I held out my pleading hands to her. But she refused to cuddle me for about five minutes. So I learned my lesson.

As I grew older my brother taught me all manner of things. We started gentle, wrestling, then ball games which turned into cricket and football, when I was old enough to accompany him to the nearby Plashet Park. I used to walk on my own when I was five, through this park to my first school, Milton High School.

My brother left the school in the term before I joined it. I well remember being taken to the school on his last day to meet the Principal Miss May L Dean. She looked at me and said, 'Your brother was a good boy and I hope you will be the same.' I must have looked a little uncertain so she asked me, 'Ken is not a bad boy is he?' I thought for a moment, then said, 'Yes!' The formidable Miss Dean was shocked as was my mother . I was also upset and endeavoured to explain that I agreed with her statement, 'Ken is not a bad boy' so I said, ''Yes'. I maintained my reply was correct despite my mother's and the Principal's arguments. It was some months before I got used to answering 'double negative' questions.

It was a strict but happy school. After doing a test or exercise, we were supposed to sit up with folded arms! I enjoyed my primary school years. [My mother recorded that I gained "9 silver medals for top boy" and also came tenth in the East Ham Scholarship Examination. This enabled me to take up a part-fee paying scholarship at any of the secondary schools around (including Brentwood). I eventually chose Wanstead County High School because my brother went there.]

I have been straying from my earliest memories. I must now confess my first deliberate and deceitful sin at the age of three or four. Every Christmas my parents hosted a family party that lasted until mid-night. My mother said I must sleep for a couple of hours otherwise I would be too tired to stay up for the party. So I was put upstairs to bed and Mum said I must not get up until the clock on the mantelpiece showed four p.m. She pointed to the hour hand and showed me exactly where that was. I protested that I would not get tired, but she was very firm that I must rest.

You can imagine how frustrated I was in the middle of Christmas excitements, to be stuck in my bedroom. For a while I tossed around unable to sleep. I kept on looking at the clock to see how much longer I had to go. It was agony.

Suddenly a wicked thought came into my mind. The clock face had no glass. The hour hand was now on three. Dare I? There was only a small gap between three and four. I crept out of bed, reached up and pulled the hour hand down to four.. I rushed back to bed and called out to Mum. She came up to tell me to try and get back to sleep. But I pointed to the clock and said, "Look - it's on four."

She was bewildered for about thirty seconds. Then her face hardened. "Did you move the clock hand ?" she demanded.

"No," I said as innocently as I could manage with reddening cheeks. It was my first deliberate lie to my mother - God forgive me. She was VERY cross. I collapsed and humbly admitted my guilt. While there is a semi-comic aspect to it, I have never forgotten this shameful episode.

Me and brother Ken in his new Wanstead County High School blazer

Chapter 2

Under the staircase of our house was first a small cupboard, then round the corner a plain wooden door. I was strictly forbidden to open it and go down the steep narrow stairs to the cellars below.

I think I should now a give brief description of our house at that time . It was a terrace house of typical design of the very early 1900's in East London (pre-World War One). There were three bedrooms and a bath room (but no toilet) on the upper floor. The ground floor had a kitchen/living room and attached scullery with a copper washing basin, gas cooker and sink. There were also two reception rooms connected by folding doors. These could be opened to make one big room for Christmas or other special occasions. The flush toilet was outside the house in a small yard before the start of a narrow garden. So at bed-time we all had to use chamber pots (jerries). But the special plus feature, according to my Dad, were the two large cellars. The first was completely given over to the receipt and storage of coal for our domestic fires. The second was my Dad's special workshop. I will describe his activities later. Originally we had gas lighting but I well remember the change to electricity. My mother was given an electric vacuum cleaner and the noise terrified me. It took me ages to get over this fear.

I think I was probably five when I was first allowed to open the forbidden door and go down into the coal cellar. There under the coal chute was an untidy mass of irregular lumps of coal, The whole cellar was thick with black dust, except for a small swept path leading to a door to the second cellar, my Dad's workshop. Some of the larger pieces of coal had shiny faces on which there were fascinating impressions of ancient ferns or other plants.

The arrival of the coal cart was always an exciting event. The cart was drawn by two enormous horses with eye shades (blinkers) and hanging nose bags for their food. Just occasionally they might eject a thick yellow gush of urine and also deposit clods of horse dung on to the road.. I felt sorry for he poor horses harnessed to the heavy coal cart with their blinkered eyes. They had no option but to relieve themselves in the street with everyone watching (or shuddering).

The heavy sacks of coal were stacked upright against a central board on the cart. The coal man would knock on the door and check details of the delivery. Then he would lever up the circular iron cover which was just in front of our bay window. Going back to his cart, he would manoeuvre a sack to the edge, heave it on to his back, and proceed to empty it down the coal hole. It was very arduous manual labour for the poor coalman.

We also enjoyed daily visits from the horse drawn dairy cart. The milk would be in a big churn, from which the dairy man would fill our personal pint or half pint pewter jugs. I heard him tell my Mum that Nelly (his horse) knew all the regular customer stops in the road. So she needed very little direction.

A bonus from all the horse-drawn traffic on the roads was actually the dung or horse droppings, My Dad made up a little trolley: a wooden box with two handles mounted on small wheels. My brother and I were sent off in the early morning with the trolley and two small shovels to collect dung for him. We really enjoyed that except when it was wet. We might see a cart going round the corner and dash hopefully after it. Dad was pleased if we managed to get a good load for he needed manure for his allotment as well as our garden.. He some times took us to his allotment (some distance away). We did token weeding and then tended to play around.

Ralph Henry Hitchcock Acton – my Dad

My Dad worked as a clerical/executive in the old Custom House in the City. He was a skilled amateur carpenter, making shelves and big items in his cellar workshop, such as the splendid oak sideboard that eventually ended up in my brother's house and was much admired. He was skilled in the photography of his day, turning his cellar into a dark room and processing the glass plates to produce lovely photos. I remember seeing large stacks of used glass plates on his shelves. He also made early wireless sets using kits from simple crystal sets to early valve hook-ups. I remember hearing 'Station 2LO' being announced on the air. He mended our shoes and boots also in his cellar. He bought sheets of leather and cut them to size with a very sharp knife. He used an iron 'last' with three foot shapes which he passed on to me in later life. And, of course, he did all the painting and paper-hanging needed for the house. Cementing was yet another skill he acquired.

While on the subject of my Dad's practical skills, largely connected with the cellar, I remember I was gradually allowed to use the work-bench and vice when I was old enough to start carpentry. But earlier than that when I was aged 7/8, I started making iron filings under the direction of brother Ken. As November 5th approached Ken started making fireworks in the shed at the bottom of our garden. We (for I was enlisted to help) rolled thin card or paper into stout tubes to fill with firework mixture. I dare not tell you the ingredients - it must be illegal to-day.

My brother needed lots of iron filings so as to enhance the fiery display when lit. It took me hours of hard filing a bar of iron held in a vice down in Dad's cellar, to make a reasonable amount of filings for his needs. It was a common practice for boys to make up a dummy Guy Fawkes on a small hand cart or push chair. They then went down the High Street asking people to 'Give a penny for the Guy.' Needless to say this was not allowable for us.

On November the 5th we had a glorious view from the back bedroom windows of all the bonfires, fireworks and parties being held in the neighbours' back gardens. On Nov,. 6th we went and bought a few fireworks, especially rockets which we could not make ourselves,. Generally we paid only half-price or less by that date. On Nov., 7th we held our own bonfire with our own and bought fireworks. Sorry if this all sounds rather mean but in those days there was little loose change to go around. For example we could not afford toilet paper . My Dad would cut newspaper into small squares, pin them together at one end, so we could tear off what was required for personal use.

Chapter 3

Only this morning eating breakfast at our ancient table, I recalled a vision of my brother aged six or seven, sitting naked on the edge of the table. He was being washed by my mother. At the time I would have been on the floor near the iron kitchen stove, awaiting my turn. I think it must have been the first time I had seen him with a bare bottom and was fascinated. Our upstairs bathroom lacked hot water as well as no toilet. For our weekly bath, it was necessary to take kettles of hot water up the stairs. So most mornings, my mother would put some warm water into a bowl on the table, sit me on one end, with legs dangling, and wash me.

Our kitchen table has so many associated memories for me. About five years old I was given the job of sweeping the crumbs off with an old brass covered brush and matching brass pan.

[Do you believe me when I tell you that, nigh on ninety years later, I still get to do the same job with the same antique brush and pan and table - only the cloth is new. Also in our larger living room we always have the table centre section in place. But unlike my Dad, I do all my carpentry on this sturdy deal table. For example, I have made and fitted wooden book-shelves in every room in our present house. As fast as I made them, my wife Doreen went out and filled them up with second-hand classics. The table surface is thus engrained with a variety of scratches. I have preserved this historic patina with two or three coats of polyurethane varnish. But I must apologise for this lengthy digression in praise of our precious old table.]

Mum, me and Ken

I had various childish ailments such as chicken-pox etc. - nothing very serious. But shortly after I had started school aged five, I began to feel very feverish, hot, head aching and painful swollen legs. I was put to bed and the Doctor called out. I was told that I had a rheumatic fever and must stay in bed until it subsided. I was later told that I needed to rest afterwards for some weeks, as undue exercise could harm my heart.

So a downstairs bed was arranged for me in that special 'front room' that was ordinarily kept 'spic and span' for visitors. At first I felt very ill with the fever and could not eat, only sip a little liquid. After a few days, I remember waking up with no head-ache but feeling weak and hungry. As my mother came into the room, I asked her whether I could have something to eat. I can still see her joyful smile as she quickly asked me what would I like.

"Could I have a piece of bread and butter with marmalade ?" I answered.

"Yes, of course, Dear." she answered, giving me a hug.

That was only the beginning of my recovery. My legs were still red and swollen. There were several weeks to endure, lying in that front room bed and missing school. To pass the time I was given early readers and illustrated fairy tales. I think I must have been given quite a lot of attention by my mother, but can remember very little of that time. But I do have a distinct memory of one picture. It showed storks flying at chimney level in some foreign country. But strangely, each stork was carrying a tiny baby wrapped in a cloth suspended from its long beak. My mother said that was how babies arrived in homes in that country. She did not seem very sure of the detail of this as I questioned her.

'Where do babies come from?' was a very big unanswered problem in my mind. I used to pester my Dad for an answer. He stoutly maintained that babies were born 'under a gooseberry bush'. I sensed he was teasing me. I argued sensibly that it would be too prickly and pointed to our own bushes. I could get no help from
my brother on this subject. When I got back to school after my lengthy illness, I soon got the answer. One of the boys my age gave me a crude simple description of the facts. (I remember his actual words but omit them as they might give offence.) I learnt that the baby grew in the woman's tummy. When it was big enough, it came

out of her tummy. I was thunderstruck and wondered whether the stork or gooseberry bush were not better ideas. Did I really grow in Mum's tummy and come out of it? But with the help of Christmas carols and the Gospel stories, I gradually got used to the idea and realised why my parents were coy about the matter. So I stopped asking questions. In those days of long maternity frocks, children were kept in 'a state of innocence', I think it was called, for as long as possible. Might we have gone too far in the other direction these days?

Following my serious illness it was decided that I ought to have my tonsils cut out as a protection against other infections taking a hold. This involved a one night stay in a hospital for the operation. I struggled against the chloroform mask, but in a few seconds I yielded not to blackness, but to a vision of a room papered with row upon row of imitation green dragons. Disturbing but not frightening. I was sore when I 'woke up' and was not happy with toilet in bed and other embarrassments. I was so pleased when Mum collected me. I believe they said, 'I had been a good boy. '

Back at Milton High School, I was doing well now, except that the teacher had to move me to the front of the class. It was short sight probably inherited from my father. My brother already had glasses and, to my sorrow, I was also doomed to become 'Four-eyes' in schoolboy parlance, for the rest of my life. Our local optician was Mr Olney, a charming man whom we saw regularly for the rest of our stay in Manor Park.. On one occasion brother Ken and I boarded the tram at Wanstead Flats and found him sitting nearby. When the conductor came by, Mr Olney insisted on buying two 'tuppeny' tickets for us, despite the fact that we needed only penny tickets to get to our home in Byron Avenue. We both agreed Mr Olney was a lovely gentleman.

Glasses reminds me of another matter, which disturbed my Mum particularly. Ken and I played happily together for most of the time, but we loved wrestling. In the schoolboy code at this time (including secondary school), wrestling was fine but arm-twisting or punching was way out of line. Ken, being so much bigger, could easily over-power me at first. But I learnt a lot and my puny muscles benefited hugely from the practice. This was a great help to me later on when I had no big brother protection. My mother very much disliked our fighting and sometimes petty quarrels. She would often tell us to stop fighting or else she would tell our father when he came home from work. Things got really bad one day, when our expensive spectacles got broken. Dad was annoyed and we had a stern lecture, but no other punishment. From that day on, Ken and I agreed always to say to each other, "Glasses off ! " before starting a wrestling bout.

On another occasion I was playing in our garden,, bouncing a golf ball dangerously close to a kitchen window. I think Ken had probably warned me, but suddenly the ball crashed through the glass! My brother was really terrified. What would Dad say ? I claimed it was an accident, but not very hopefully. Mum was very concerned. When Dad came in, she told him. He was cross and warned me never to do it again. Then that weekend my clever Dad measured up the window, stripped out the broken glass and old putty and went and bought replacement glass. Then he showed us how he fitted and puttied in the new glass.

In retrospect I think my Dad was a 'softie'. Certainly a patient man on the evidence above. Ken and I were fortunate to have such loving and capable parents.

Chapter 4   Indoor play-time.

I believe I had an ancient Teddy at one time. But this somehow turned into a bedraggled Golly (black rag doll). I soon forgot them in favour of wooden bricks. I would build small forts or castles and place my lead soldiers in position. I had been given a small spring-loading cannon which would fire a sizeable wooden shell. I confess I loved shooting shells at the hapless soldiers and knocking the forts to a shambles with great glee. There was a degree of skill involved. An excellent game which I can recommend for children, if only they can get hold of a decent cannon.

Following on the wooden bricks, came Meccano, a major educational toy. I was always happy with this - see the early picture in Chapter One of Ken and myself with a Meccano model, my Mother watching while preparing the vegetables on our historic kitchen table. I used to save my pennies to add to my Meccano collection. I liked buying long bars to make big cars, etc. My best model was of a hammerhead crane mounted on wheels. I loved getting on my knees to push it all round the room by steering the cab. It would be about 18 inches tall and tended to over-balance when turning corners at 'speed'. This aroused parental concern. I studied the problem and proudly produced my original solution. I put in an extra pair of wheels with an over-long axle in the middle of the chassis. As I turned the crane on a right-hand bend, the middle wheels naturally veered to the left propping up the side which had a tendency to topple over. This was a great success. I asked my Dad whether I could get a patent for my invention. He merely smiled and gave me a pat on the back.

We also had basic train sets with clockwork engines. The best fun (though we did not really know this at the time) came from building up the inter-locking sets of rails, plus working in a couple of points and a cross-over.

My brother Ken rigged up a telephone connection between our two bed-rooms. He used the two ear pieces from an old head-set he had somehow acquired. He did this shortly after we were separated from sleeping in twin beds in the large back bedroom. My father gave up his hobby of breeding canaries in the whole of the middle bedroom. I only remember once seeing the floor to ceiling cage. This allowed my move to the 'canary room'. I began to miss my brother's company, so his telephone idea was a brilliant solution. Furthermore Ken had got hold of a wireless set, probably a crystal set, and began sending me exciting radio programmes. I well remember one. It was a drama series featuring Dr Fu Man Chu. The radio was stopped after a while, but the telephone link was allowed for quite a time.

Music. I expect those who know me, will be expecting this subject. I have already mentioned my mother's lovely and expert piano playing. The piano was a French Thibouville-Lamy upright. It was kept in the front parlour, placed against the inner party wall of our hall. This was so as to minimise noise offence to our terrace neighbours. So long as I did not bang the keys with my fist or any object, I was allowed to use my fingers on it. I used to pretend I was playing, but no real music emerged from my scribbling.

When I was about four or five, I was allowed to use our wind-up portable gramophone. I was carefully shown how to allow the pick-up arm and needle to drop very gently on the outer rim, so as to get a hum before the music started. There was a great danger of scratching the record, if the process was not done properly. Otherwise the record would be spoilt. I think I was allowed several tries on an already spoilt record. But I became qualified to put on records of all kinds by myself. That Christmas I was given an HMV set of nursery rhymes in a special cardboard container, which I still keep as a souvenir. One song I specially liked was 'Laughing Ginger Brown'. The chorus was something like, 'Ha ha ha ha ,ha ha ha ha, He, he he he he,' screeching up and down . You can imagine my rendering, applauded when first sung, soon became annoying. Another pop song of this period, but not in my junior 7 inch diameter records, was 'Goosey Goo'. In our Plashet Park was a bandstand from which one could hear military bands or small variety ensembles. That is where I heard something like, 'When ever I see you, my heart goes Goosey, goosey , goosey goosey, goo!'

As well as listening, I liked to dance to the music and also noisily sing at times. Imitating a screechy operatic Soprano once, I saw my Mum and faltered to a stop. 'Do go on . That's quite good !', she said to my amazement. I remember singing once at a Milton High School concert for parents. I was asked to sing 'Soup of the evening, beautiful soup,' the Mock Turtle's song by Lewis Carroll. I was encouraged to screech it up and down, dragging each word out slowly in mournful fashion. This caused great fun, hearty applause from the audience and boosted my ego.

Outdoor Activities

The convenience of being close to Plashet Park cannot be under-estimated. It was safe and from the age of five, I walked through it to school every day. I could play with Ken, school friends or boys I did not know. The camaraderie (a word I didn't know then) was really great. If I was alone or with two or three friends, we could hang around on the edge of a game of football. Within minutes, a break would occur and the Captains would assign us to a place in their teams. Exactly the same would happen with scratch games of cricket, usually played with a tennis ball against a chalk-marked wicket on one of the trees lining the central pathway through the Park. Brother Ken taught me how to do over-arm bowling, especially off-breaks, which was a useful gift when I started secondary school cricket.

I was not allowed a cycle in Manor Park. The High Street trams ran on surface land rails with dangerous ruts which were a trap for cycle wheels. Cost may also have been a factor. However I was allowed a scooter when I was maybe eight or nine. This became my pride and joy. I loved walking it (maybe just a little glide when no one was watching) a few yards down Byron Avenue and then across one quiet road to the Park entrance.

Once inside I could speed away with joyous ease. A favourite route was a round trip. I would go left from the entrance and then down and up a very large dip. This was supposed to have been caused by a Zeppelin bomb from World War One. Gradually turning right I would come to the outdoor Bowls Club, a favourite with my Dad and my Grandfather. Going on to the far corner I would reach the Public Library of great interest to me at a later age. Then turning right I would reach the far exit that led to my school. Crossing the main central avenue to the far right corner were the grass courts of the Tennis Club. My Dad and Mum were both members in my very early days. Coming back on the central avenue, I would pass the Band Stage and so reach the Byron Avenue entrance. Then I might decide to try a few trips up and down the 'bomb hole' to see how fast I could go. Or maybe I might spot a lively game of football and wait for the invitation to join in.

We usually had a two weeks summer sea-side holiday. I can recall Weymouth, Isle of Wight (once) and more often Walton on the Naze. Some times my Dad would leave us for a week because of office work. We built sand castles, netted shrimps and crabs, paddled and attempted swimming (if it was warm enough) in our flimsy cotton one-piece swimming costumes.

My Dad was keen that we should learn to swim. So when I was nine or ten, he took Ken and me from home on early morning swimming expeditions. Setting out around 7 a.m., we went by tram to Wanstead Flats and then a long walk to Wanstead Park, where there was early morning swimming in one of the lakes. It was strictly reserved only for men and boys and finished sharply at 8a.m. It was not too deep and I could stand up and pretend to be doing my breast stroke. I was keen to learn. At home I used to balance on my tummy over the piano stool and practice my arms and leg-kicks. The next summer when I was ten, I bravely took my feet off the bottom and swam a few strokes. I was so pleased as was my Dad. As the finishing time of 8 a.m. approached there would be a desperate flurry of mainly men to get in past the Keeper on duty. There seemed to be no rule about wearing a costume, although we and most people did. I remember seeing one or two desperate late-comers rushing in at two minutes to eight, flinging off their clothes wildly and jumping naked into the water.

Chapter 5 Grandparents

Grandfather, Grandmother Acton and son, my Uncle Edgar

My paternal grandparents also lived in Byron Avenue at No.146   This was quite a distance from the Plashet Park end where we lived at No. 12.

My grandfather, John Henry Hitchcock Acton, was a very lively character who, despite little formal education, had worked his way up in Slazengers (the Sports firm) to become Works Manager. He and his father, John Elon Hitchcock, were recruited by Ralph Slazenger at the very beginning of the famous firm, for their skill in bentwood furniture making.

On 21.1.1904 my grandfather, described as a Tennis Bat Maker (sic), was made a Freeman of the City of London. At the same time he changed his name by deed poll by adding Acton at the end of his previous name, John Henry Hitchcock..

Because we lived so near, I often saw him and he would tease me a little - ask me how I was getting on with my Gazinters (a crude reference to division sums). He would ask about school and also boast about how Suzanne Lenglen (the French tennis star) insisted that he must personally string her tennis racquets. [Just a few years ago, we discovered that my grandfather had patented an improved racquet, with additional layers in the connection between head and handle, so as to give greater flexibility in action. This almost certainly helped Suzanne win Wimbledon in the early Twenties.]

I saw less of his wife (formerly Alice Crook) as she died in 1936. My one particular early memory was being taken down to see her by my Dad. She was a very large lady sitting in an arm chair. She chatted and smiled at me. Then she said to Dad, "Look at his heavy shoes, Ralph. You ought to buy him a nice pair of light shoes."

I felt sorry for my Dad, knowing how hard he worked in the cellar, mending all our family shoes with good stout leather, and giving a smart finish with some sort of special sealing wax. So I waggled my feet and said, "My shoes are fine."

There followed some friendly arguments between my Dad and Grandmother. I remember no more except that I had a strong impression that my Dad was pleased with me.

My Mother's parents were George Hare Bates (Farvie) and Anna Elizabeth Bates (formerly Best).

They were married at Islington in 1885. I did not know my grandfather George Hare Bates, as I understand he died a few months after I was born. But when grandmother Bates came to live near us when I was about eight I think, I formed a very strong attachment to Nan as I called her. I loved her dearly.

Mrs Anna Elizabeth Bates (formerly Best)

Nan lived in a rented room sometimes as close as No.10 Byron Avenue. Apart from clothes, all her possessions were in a suitcase under her bed. I could visit her on my own and she would show me her treasures, mostly old photos of her family, some in uniforms of the first World War, and a special pet sheep dog with woolly hair all over its face. She would often visit our home and sometimes mind me; if need be. She had very litle money and existed on a small pension. Yet she gave us generous presents. I had a lovely illustrated educational book given me each Christmas. It was usually one of "The Wonder Book" series with funny Heath Robinson drawings on the end papers..

She also told me stories from her early life in Sturminster Newton. How her father, a GPO worker, caught trout in the streams. Sometimes he would see Thomas Hardy, the famous novelist, out walking. Thomas was no snob and would say the odd word to her father when they passed by. She also gave me an agonising account of what happened when her father shaved at the kitchen table, with all the family sitting round in a deadly hush. No one dare make a cough or fidget in case the sharp razor slipped. That was one of her early memories.

My Nan was very faithful in visiting family graves in the City of London Cemetry just by the Wanstead Flats.. In the Autumn she would come back from such a visit with a load of lovely shiny conkers concealed in a large handbag. She said that collecting them was against the rules, but she knew I would like them .

Chapter 6 First Piano Lessons.

Much to my surprise, my Mother did not give my first piano lessons. She tried just once, I think to give me the basic note names on the ledger lines. Then she felt it would be better if I had a proper teacher. So she engaged a pleasant young lady, Miss Doris Long, to give me a weekly half-hour lesson. There is some doubt about the date, but I think I was just eight at the time. This went quite well for a few months, until I began to get tired of the daily practice involved. I thought of giving up and confided in my Mum. She was very gentle and sympathetic, but encouraged me to give it another try . So to please her, I tried harder to improve. I gradually got better and even enthusiastic! I would try playing the C Major scale with my fingers on the breakfast table cloth.

I did so well that it was suggested (by my teacher or Mum?) that I should enter a local piano competition. My memory is now validated by hard evidence. It was called an EISTEDDFORD, held at the United Methodist Church, Katherine Road, Forest Gate, E7 and I won my very first certificate (Third Class) on 31 May 1930 at the age of Nine and a half.. The Adjudicator was Doris Hill LRAM,ARCM. I also have her report where she noted 'Fingers too flat, good start, poor middle section but good on the whole plus a recommendation to study touch.' She gave me 75 marks out of 100.

It was a very accurate assessment - my touch needed expert tuition. I use to love trying to play quickly, but the fingers in my hand would tense and cramp up badly.

Miss Long did her best but my progress was erratic.

I believe it was that Summer that my mother and I went for a few days on a trial holiday. We took a train to Clacton and then a short bus ride South to the village of St. Osyth (locally known as Toosey). We stopped for two or three nights in a rented upper room in an ordinary house. We shared the house toilet but had to wash in our bedroom using a wash bowl and water jug on a side table. Our objective was the St, Osyth beach chalets some two and a half miles away: a long walk there and back each day. We visited a previously contacted chalet (wooden beach bungalow) to see whether this form of holiday would suit for our family holiday. I tried out the swimming from a sandy beach which was good. However, I remember being embarrassed by having to change in the kitchen with no privacy. We gave Dad a good report and I think we booked for week's holiday in August staying at a rented chalet.

My mother's illness. In the Summer of 1931, I think it was, my mother developed a severe illness affecting her gall bladder. A difficult removal operation was safely achieved , but Mum needed a few weeks of recuperation in a nursing home at Walton on the Naze (on the cliffs at the Naze end). My grandmother, Nan, was asked to look after me. Further and excitingly more, Nan took me to stay at her sister's boarding house in the prestigious Prittlewell Square in Southend on Sea.

I shared with my Nan a ground-floor room and bed at the back of the main house, just by the tradesman entrance. I was instructed to call her sister (the owner) Auntie Annie. She was a live-wire little lady dressed in black with a high lace band propped around her neck. In earlier days she had acted as a Nanny to the children of various well-to-do people. Some of these contacts were now her long-term paying guests. She seemed very much in control of her business.

She was old-fashioned (as also was my Nan) and kept a pet talking parrot in her kitchen near he back door. I often heard her talking to it. One morning, just as I was getting up, I heard and saw the baker enter and knock on Auntie's kitchen door just ajar.

"Not to-day, thank you," I heard Auntie say. But later on, I heard Auntie asking my Nan if she had seen the baker call as she needed a loaf. I quickly said I had heard Auntie say "Not to-day, thank you." There was an explosion of laughter as we realised that the parrot was to blame. Apparently this was not the first time it had happened.

I liked the gardens and band-stand in the square. I also remembered the piles of spent tea leaves in the back garden. This was because interesting colonies of black ants nesting amongst them.

Unfortunately Aunt Annie had no piano available for me to play. But she liked talking to me. Once she   produced a few pictures (classical prints) to show me. One had lots of cherubs dancing around in the nude. "Are they not naughty boys to go around without clothes?" she asked me mischievously.

"Oh – Annie !" gasped my Nan in embarrassment.

I wondered what to say so mumbled, " I don't think so." The subject was quickly dropped. I remembered Nan taking me to the local cinema in Manor Park once. In the interval between the main picture and B Movie, there used to be a short live performance of some sort. On that occasion a row of dancing girls came on. They all wore shorts and were quite decent in my opinion. But my Nan was really upset which puzzled me. [When a few years later I played piano in the 1937 film "Talking Feet," where there were two or more lines of high-kicking girls, I shudder to think what my Nan would have thought if she had seen it.]

My Southend holiday soon finished following my mother's successful recuperation and return home. But she had to take things easily and not do too much walking.

Our first car. My brilliant and loving Dad decided that Mum now deserved a car. Firstly he engaged a Mr Wright, who owned a Riley, to give my Mum driving lessons. Then, probably on his advice, Dad bought her a second-hand baby Austin Seven saloon with number plate, "VX 8181". Within a month or two, for there were no driving tests required then, we were all being driven around to exciting places. Mum was at the wheel, Dad alongside and Ken and I squashed in the back seats with spare luggage. I think Ken was all right but I had to learn to cope with car sickness. The car was kept in a garage space at the back of the grocers on the High Streeet corner as it intersected Byron Avenue. The grocery was famed for supplying kittens for anyone who needed them (not us). Also they would give a penny for returned empty bottles and sell broken biscuits at a cheap price.

Strangely my Dad, despite his all-round skills in carpentry, DIY, photography and office work never took up driving. My Mum, however, soon became a good and confident driver. The nearest she came to an 'incident' was when she followed a tram at the High Street and Romford Road intersection. She suddenly discovered that tramway workmen had cut away the tarmac inter-fill between the rails ! There was no warning and the little Austin Seven wheels bumped crazily about eight inches up and down, with us perforce doing the same. But Mum kept her nerve, did not stop and carried on to the Wanstead Flats. Some folk have made fun of the baby Austin Seven, calling it within my hearing, as little more than a motorised pram. But it did us very well and could reach 40 mph on a level clear road.

Reverting to the subject of my piano studies, I recently rediscovered a little note book which my Mum was keeping about me. It was a brief record of my progress in music studies and also school work.. She noted that my piano lessons were very irregular. After a year or more Miss Long told Mum that I had reached her (Miss Long's) standard and needed a higher qualified teacher. Mum and I both remembered how we had been impressed by Miss Doris Hill. So Mum made enquiries at the Metropolitan Academy of Music , Forest Gate,where

Miss Hill was employed. She received a glowing testimonial. This eventually led to my becoming a pupil of Miss Doris Hill on 2ndDecember 1932. I was within ten days of my twelfth birthday and had started at Wanstead County High School the previous September. I was deemed fit to travel on my own to school and piano lessons.

[My Life Story continues in Parts 2 and 3]

My LIFE STORY PART TWO

From Dancing Fingers to Talking Feet (1932-38)

Myself on a film set when I was sixteen

Chapter 7

I well remember my first day at Wanstead County High School at the start of the school year in early September 1932. I was eleven, still in short trousers but proudly wearing the smart black regulation cap and blazer with its heron badge and Latin scroll, 'ABEUNT STUDIA IN MORES' which I was told meant, 'Studies shape the mind'. I should mention here that there was a well established colony of herons in near-by Wanstead Park. We used to see skeins of herons flying over the school from time to time. The senior boys and girls became Old Heronians when they left school.

I was not too nervous when I left home with my elder brother, Ken. He would have been at least four years at the school and would ensure I got there and help me settle into the routine. We caught the red double-decker bus (No. 101A I believe) at the high street end of our road. It went all the way to Wanstead but we got off at Overton Drive. From there we walked down it past a golf course on one side, until we reached the school. Ken then guided me into the right entrance so as to reach the main school hall, where the day started with morning prayers, a hymn and notices. I was ushered down by a prefect to stand with the other new boys and girls at the front..

On the stage were sitting a formidable array of teachers in academic gowns and the Headmaster, A F Joseph MA.
He gave us new boys and girls a warm welcome, before we had a roll call to group us in two mixed forms, each about thirty pupils strong. Then we were led off to our own regular classroom to meet our form teacher.

My first form teacher was a pleasant lady but I regret I cannot remember her name. We were a mixed bunch of boys and girls. We were each allocated individual desks. Each desk had a fitted inkwell and then a slightly sloping hinged top which opened up so we could store our pencils, pens, rulers, rubbers, etc and also exercise and text books. We were given timetables of classes in our own form room or elsewhere if need be, e.g. the weekly PE class in the gym. We were also grouped in 'Houses' right across the school range, four for boys and four for girls. We had no choice. I was made a Viking - the other possibilities were Romans, Celts or Saxons. The girls' Houses were named after trees, Beeches, Limes, Oaks and Willows.

We had another roll call by our form teacher so that she would get to know us and where each pupil sat. All boys were known just by their surname, whereas the girls were allowed a first name and then their surname. Because of this we boys generally used surnames in chats among ourselves, but could refer to girls by their Christian names.

On that first day, I was relieved to find that I could cope reasonably well with the classroom work and found it interesting. I was pleasantly surprised about eleven o'clock to find that we had a mid-morning play break of about twenty minutes. WHS claimed to be a pioneer mixed secondary school, but the boys' and girls' playgrounds were strictly segregated. This meant that we had very little opportunity to talk to the girls as chatting in class was forbidden.

It was enjoyable getting to know one another in the boys' playground and observe what the older boys were doing. Some produced tennis balls for impromptu football. There were also varied games of tag or 'It'.

The most spectacular game of all was 'Horses and Riders'. Two teams of about nine to twelve boys each were selected by captains. They tossed to see who would be the first team to be 'Riders'.

The losers had to form a long line of 'Horses'. The boys had to bend down so that their hands could grip the ankles or calves of the boy in front of them – and also jam their heads under the legs of that boy. The foremost loser boy would stand facing the line of 'Horses', with legs apart and back against a wall to withstand the pressure from the line of boys facing him. Then the first 'Rider' would take a run and make a mighty leap to land as far forward as possible onto the back of a boy-horse. The others followed one at a time, sometime landing on top of another boy-rider. The aim was to apply pressure on the line of boy-horses until it crumbled or gave way giving victory to the 'Riders'. However, if any of the 'Riders' fell off, the 'Horses' won and rapidly demanded their turn to be Riders. It was a very rough and tumble game, as I found out when I tried it at a later date. I am not aware of any serious injury resulting during my time at the School, but I doubt whether the game would pass today's safety regulations.

After break-time we had another class period before lunch-time. Most of us had pre-paid school 'dinners'. We went to the dining hall in a separate building to sit at tables holding about 12-14 pupils (all boys) with a prefect or monitor in charge at one end. I don't remember any 'lining up'. The food was brought in on trolleys. At the far end there was a High Table for the teachers. One of these would give the customary Grace of thanks for what we were about to receive. Then we could start eating. Also when we had enjoyed our second course or 'pudding', we had to wait for a second Grace - 'for what we had received', before we could dash off and enjoy the playground once more. It all sounds rather formal but quite jolly in fact. There was some naughty by-play – practical tricks on the monitor in charge (normally dealt with swiftly) and lots of lively discussions. A few weeks later, immediately after the second 'Grace', I and two or three friends used to dash madly from the dining hall to the Fives Court to book it for a game.

After the final afternoon class it was time to go home (around 4 p.m. I believe). I had told brother Ken that I was quite safe to travel back alone. This suited him as he usually travelled home with his mates. So I packed up my satchel with one or two books for the required home-work and set off. Half-way down Overton Drive, I was delighted when a boy cyclist from our form stopped to walk along with me. I think his name was Aldcroft. I caught the bus back and went triumphantly home to tell Mum what a lovely and exciting day I had enjoyed.

I was very confident walking down with Ken to catch the bus the next day. "No problems," I told him. "I can travel on my own now." So Ken decided to travel on the upper deck with his mates, while I stopped below to ensure easy departure at the Overton Drive bus stop. But when the bus duly arrived at Overton Drive, I was still day- dreaming of other things. I heard boys clattering down from the upper deck to get off and suddenly realised that it might be my stop ! I got out of my seat quickly, but too late. The bus was gathering speed and was already some distance away in unfamiliar scenery. I was really worried now. The only comfort was the knowledge that the final destination of the bus was Wanstead. Once there I could ask people the way to the school.

I left the bus accordingly at the final Wanstead stop. As I looked around for clues of where to go, I saw someone running up from where we had come. It was faithful brother Ken ! He was panting heavily and red-faced. He had run following the bus all the way from the Overton Drive bus stop. I expected a wigging. However, he was relieved that he had caught up with me and gave me only a mild rebuke.

From then on school life continued at an even pace with no significant problems. I began to make some special friends from the boys in my form. However none of these lived near me, so free time in the evening was mostly spent on homework and piano practice. The latter was specially important to me as I was looking forward to some top class tuition at the Metropolitan Academy of Music at their Forest Gate Branch, Earlham Hall. As mentioned in my 'Very earliest memories', my mother had arranged for me to start lessons with Miss Doris Hill.

Earlham Hall, 1934.

Chapter 8

On 2nd of December 1932 I went with my mother for my first lesson at Earlham Hall . I was carrying some recent pieces, scale books etc., in my Mum's old music case. It was a reasonably mild December evening, but a little foggy as we walked through the imposing front doors of the Hall. A receptionist took our details and showed us the way to Miss Hill's studio. We walked down a corridor through to the back of the building and down some steps into the garden. There through the foggy mist we could just see the outlines of what appeared to be two lines of wooden beach huts! As we made our way along the central pathway, we heard a wild cacophony of piano, violin, cello and singing, as if in a discordant welcome to our appearance. Our guide gently tapped on the door of one of the huts (I cannot recall the number). Faint piano music within stopped. Within a minute or so the door opened and a young girl came out followed by Miss Hill herself, who invited us in and greeted us warmly.

I remembered her face which I thought had a kind of classic beauty approaching that of my Mum. Her face also appeared natural with a slight sun-tan but no ugly red lipstick. She was wearing a business-like grey tweed suit.

She apologised to my Mum for the unusual studio . She said that after Christmas she hoped to rent a better studio over a music shop. The hut was actually quite cosy and warm. Miss Hill said that generally she preferred to teach the older pupils such as me (almost twelve) on their own, but Mum could stop if she wanted. I felt sure my Mum would have liked to stop, as she had studied piano herself at the elite Guildhall School of Music. Mum, putting my needs first, took the hint and left to await my return to the Hall.

At last I was sitting on the piano stool while my teacher carefully adjusted the height so that my hands were at the right level just above the keys. Then she asked me to play a piece of my own choosing. I cannot remember what I played, nor Miss Hill's exact comments. It was something like, "Good. You have improved since I last heard you play at the competition I judged. But we must work on your touch so that your fingers are more relaxed as they play each note."

Then she took hold of my right elbow with her left hand and my right wrist with her right hand. She gently tried moving my right hand back and forth above the keys. I naturally resisted this movement, but she explained that I must try and relax my elbow joint. We did this for a few times until I managed to relax sufficiently to allow her free control. Then I was asked to play a scale or a line of music while keeping my elbow and fore-arm in this relaxed state.

"Well done," she said. "Now you will be able to learn to get your fingers to dance and run across the keys, without straining and ending up in a cramp."

I tried playing another of my pieces using this relaxed technique, which I found difficult. But she encouraged me to try. After that she tested my sight-reading which was rather slow by her standards.

She said I needed to learn a few new lines of music each week. She would give me a note for my mother to buy a theory work book and a piece by C.P.E. Bach titled Solfeggietto. To whet my interest she took over the piano stool and played this Bach piece by memory. It was a continuous line of running (dare I say dancing?) music, mostly played one hand after another, but so smoothly that I could not hear the joins.

The forty minute lesson was soon over. As I left to rejoin my mother, I was enthralled, excited and determined that I would strive to learn to play as Miss Hill did.

[I followed much of Miss Hill's methods in my own piano teaching some fifty years later. I still love playing the Solfeggietto from memory at 94. I have taught many pupils to get their fingers dancing and running through this music by J.S. Bach's second son.]

Chapter 9

After this musical interlude I must get back to my description of school life in my first term at WHS. One afternoon a week we had games, usually Rugby in the Autumn and early Spring (provided it was not freezing as falling on the hard ground could be dangerous). I was disappointed as I was on the small thin size and would have preferred football.

On that first Rugby day, we changed into shorts, shirt and football boots for training on the upper field, which was equipped with the tall Rugby posts at each end. We started to learn how to throw and to catch the oval ball. "Why must it be a silly oval ball," we thought. This made kicking difficult. Then we had to try running holding the oval ball in our right arm, while being prepared to fend off potential tacklers with our left hand.

Tackling ideally involved a low dive to seize the legs, preferably the ankles, of a running player of the opposing team. It required athletic skill, careful judgment and courage to attempt this risky move. If well done the strongest player would be forced to crash down. So we started tackling practice. Everyone had to try two tackles and then experience twice being tackled. The pitch was a little muddy and we were soon muddied ourselves plus a few bruises.

Then we practised forming opposing 'scrums'. Being light, I was put in the pack of 8 'Forwards' as the 'Hooker' in the middle of our front row. The boys either side of me were my support so that my legs were free to try and heel the ball backwards, when it was flung into the middle of the scrum by our 'scrum-half'. With the opposing hooker trying to do the same thing, bruised shins were often the result. I and the other forwards alongside and behind were bent over and interlaced. Once the ball had been thrown in, the forwards (except the suspended hookers) shoved forward as hard as they could with their combined weight and strength. The hookers sought vigorously to heel the ball back to their scrum mates. If our side shoved hard enough to get possession of the ball, it would be seized by the fly-half and passed backward or level sideways (passing forward is an offence), to one of the four waiting 'Three – quarters'

The three quarters were the elite, chosen for their speed and vigour. They were the ones to run and feint, carrying the ball with the aim of touching it down just over the line of the enemy's ground, preferably near to the goal posts to get a TRY. It might then be converted to a goal by one of our players who was a good kicker,

Forwards could also sometimes score a try or even kick a goal in mid-play. I think that I only ever scored two TRYS in my five years at the school. There were a lot more complicated rules about knock-ons and line-outs, etc., but I fear I have already bored my readers on this subject.

Getting back to my first afternoon of Rugby training, our group of muddied boys needed to wash or shower before resuming normal school clothing. I was very shy at this stage of my life and did not fancy going naked with other boys into the communal shower. They were packed in tightly and a fantastic sight. The master in charge soon shut the doors to give the group some freedom from our gaping eyes. I cleaned myself using an ordinary wash basin. A few months later, individual showers were installed and I finally dared to use one.

Our weekly PE in the gym also required changing into our kit, but showers were deemed unnecessary. We did ladder-work, rope climbing and jumping over the 'horse' using a spring board plus other exercises. I managed an A1 certificate for the first year, but failed the next year because they raised the height of the horse too much for my short height. In trying to clear the end of the horse during a 'long-fly', I strained my back, which annoyed me as unfair and harmful.

In the Summer term we often had swimming in our unheated outdoor pool in lieu of PE in the gym. There was also sometimes athletic training and cross-country running. The latter usually went through Wanstead Park. On one occasion we had to run also through the River Roding, getting soaked at waist level! I was better at cross-country than sprinting. I borrowed from my piano technique to learn to run in a relaxed manner, synchronising my breathing in time with my running paces. This enabled me to improve my stamina. In the big race (all the lower school) where we got wet crossing the river Roding, I managed to come in about 5th or $6^{th,}$ although I was sick before it finished. Unfortunately it was filmed and shown to the whole school on one occasion: I was shown vomiting as I carried on gamely to try and preserve my position and earn points for my Viking House.

However, our main game was now cricket, much to my delight. My training and practice in Plashet Park was a useful preparation, even though we used a hard cricket ball rather than the softer tennis ball I had previously used. I mentioned earlier that brother Ken had taught me how to bowl 'off-spinners'. Apparently my expertise in this form of bowling was considered good enough to earn me a place eventually in the Viking House cricket team,

The first match I played, maybe against the Saxons, was rather an ordeal. As the youngest and smallest I batted last. When I was called in to take my centre bearing from the umpire at the far end, I had to face four balls to complete the over before the bowling switched to the other end. I was fourteen I think, and the Saxon bowler was a hefty sixth former! My captain had urged me to let alone any ball not in line with the wicket. The first ball raced by on the off side – good. The second ball was closer in line with the off stump and very fast. I bravely tried to block it, but the ball knocked my bat backwards and continued with a slight deflection past the wicket-keeper towards the boundary! I had started to run, but no need –I had scored four runs. However, I was out next ball to a yorker knocking down my middle stump. Now it was our turn to bowl and field. I was placed some distance from the action and allowed just one over near the end. I am rather vague about the result. I was nervous and not too accurate at first, so boundaries were being scored. But I managed one really good off -break which resulted in a slip catch to my delight.

Chapter 10

I must now try to introduce some of the boys (and maybe girls) and the teachers. I had no photos of year one but found an excellent form photo of my second year:-

WCHS Form Photo 1933

Our Form teacher, Mr K.B.Swaine with his 31 pupils, 13 of whom were girls. He was also a specialist Maths teacher and a strong disciplinarian, but very fair. So there was no playing about in his lessons. We respected him even though we gave him a nick-name – not difficult to guess (just omit the a from his surname). Towards the end of my secondary school life, he wrote me a farewell letter. Knowing my interest in classical music, he made amusing comments such as the waste of so many orchestral players of the same instrument, when all that was needed was one player of each kind with a microphone, to produce sufficient volume for any large hall. I thought he could have added that a purer sound could then well emerge (undoubtedly in school orchestras) as in a string quartet. He also admitted the genius of the great composers but added, "They never knew when to stop." This was only gentle fun at my expense in a very encouraging letter. [Years later I discovered that the basic school maths text-books that helped my youngest son do well, were by K.B. Swaine.]

You might be asking where are all the smart school blazers with the Heron crest? The requirement had been dropped to save expense for parents, probably due to our kindly Headmaster, Mr A.F.Joseph,

Individual boys.

Middle Row – I am on the extreme left with best friend Grave alongside. We got on well at first until we had a playground dispute over a broken ruler belonging to Grave. He claimed it was my fault and wanted to break mine. I denied the charge and felt it would be silly to end up with two broken rulers. He tried to grab mine and I resisted firmly. It soon turned into a furious wrestling match. Neither would give way and the fight carried on until the bell sounded for end of the break. "We have wasted the whole break on this silly quarrel," I said. "Can't we shake hands and forget it? You can have my ruler if you want." He smiled and offered his hand saying, "All right – you can keep your ruler." That's how we became close friends. We loved dashing out from lunch, after the second grace, to play fives or whatever games were available. We would sit together on school coach excursions, such as a visit to the Rothampstead Research Institute on trees and plants. He even sometimes chanced finding me at home, by travelling on his own from his home at 54 Wellesley Road Ilford to mine in Manor Park to play (as he put it). I am sorry to say that I only once attempted a return visit, by an arrangement to play billiards I had other things to do normally, piano practice, excursions with brother Ken, or car trips with my parents.

The only other boy, whose address I recorded in my earliest diary (1935) was H.Greenburg,, who lived at 81 Headley Drive, Ilford. He was a year or more younger than the rest of us, as you can see from the photo where he is placed with Goldburg. Both boys are squatting on the ground, Greenburg to the left. Greenburg became a special friend. He was extremely bright to have passed either a scholarship or entry exam, to have gained a start at WHS so early. He was very keen to do well and we competed some times for the top place in form tests. He was proud of his Jewish faith and would tell me of the arduous study he had to undertake towards getting accepted for his Bar Mitzvah.

The sturdy boy on the left of the top row was Osborne who took a friendly interest in me. He was a good all-rounder in games (Rugby, etc.) and form work. He used to quiz me about my home life, asking such questions as whether I washed in cold water in getting up in the morning – I did and thought nothing special in that. He also tested my knowledge on sexual matters which was minimal. I think he was one of a number of better-off form members whose homes had a telephone: they used to phone one another of an evening to discuss the homework required. The boy next to Osborne was probably Inson. Further to the right of the three girls in the top row were Cross and Russell, all worthy solid characters.

There are many familiar faces in the middle row but my memory of their names is weak. Starting from the right, the second boy is Aldcroft who cycled to school and sometimes walked with me along Overton Drive. He even let me try riding his cycle once or twice. I was unskilled but avoided falling off. To the left of Aldcroft was Bennett, a gentle friendly boy who some times got bullied. It was rumoured that he was not strong and might have only one functioning kidney.

When I look at the girls, I can remember some of the faces but names escape me, except for one . I think she is probably in the front row of girls, second starting from the left of the photo.

Chapter 11 - Bullying

Generally, with one shocking exception, I think very little bullying went on. In my very early days at the school I was very shocked and frightened by a commotion in the boys' cloakroom, going home time. There on the floor was a small naked boy crying piteously while two or three very senior six-formers were making fun of him. There was a crowd of boys watching this cruelty, but no one daring to try and stop the big bullies. One of the bullies picked up the naked little boy, held him up high and whirled him around the room for general viewing. I felt a cold chill within at seeing such unchecked evil. I ran off home. I think I told Ken but not my parents. Ken told me later that there were two or three expulsions, almost certainly resulting from this affair.

In that first year, I suffered only a very minor incident. I went to the boys' toilets and was suddenly pushed into a cubicle by two boys not much older than myself. They were behind me so I could only catch odd glimpses of their faces They were intent on taking down my short trousers and pants. I resisted strongly for about five minutes before they succeeded in seeing my 'willy'. I was fearing pinching or worse, but one of them said, " I just like to see it". Then they suddenly released me and ran off. I told Ken but not my parents. Ken said I ought to report them, but I could not identify them and it never happened again.

One day I was going home rather late, when I came across Bennett being bullied by three boys in the school drive, just outside the cloakroom He was yelling for help. They were trying to induce an ant or two to go down his neck. I called them to stop and made brief sallies to try and get Bennett's release without being caught myself. Then I looked around and went off to get help. But it was late and I could not find anybody. When I finally went home the drive was deserted. I realised then that I had behaved cowardly and let Bennett down. I should have been bolder and plunged fighting into the group, even if they had let Bennett go and started on me. I apologised humbly to Bennett the next day, but he rightly refused to speak to me or allow a resumption of friendship. The shame of this incident remains with me to the present day.

Chapter 12 - Progress in school work and piano

My mother's notebook on school work from exams in Feb 1933 to December 1934 show a succession of 1st places plus two form prizes. She gave up this record to concentrate on my piano progress in exams and competitions. What an odious child I was! I did not mind if I was called a 'swot', a derogatory label for a boy. I enjoyed most of the school work, although weak on Geography and History.

But I was fascinated by piano playing and my lessons with Miss Hill. You may recall I described her first lesson with me in some detail in Chapter 8. Her teaching went beyond the paid-for weekly lessons. She would organise extra groups to learn theory and give extra coaching at times at her home at 22 Park Road, Wanstead, where she lived with an aging aunt. Some times there were advanced pupils there to practice a performance on her Bechstein boudoir grand-piano. She would sit beside me so I could overcome shyness. Also I well remember I once went to her house with a streaming cold. She produced a small bottle of TCP and made me gargle and also sniff it up my nostrils – then gave me the bottle to take home. This was a new remedy for my Mum and she was duly grateful to Miss Hill.

But what happened on my second and subsequent lessons with Miss Hill ? She almost certainly started my preparation for the first formal M.A.M examination for their Bronze Medal. I passed this with 88 % marks in December 1933.

In the Spring of 1934, Miss Hill arranged for me to play piano duets with another of her pupils, Yvonne Thurley who was about my age. This was quite fun. We gained a Certificate of Merit First Class in the Stratford competition for 13 to 16 years, and won the First Prize in the MAM annual competition for 13-15 years. Unfortunately the latter achievement required us to play at the MAM prize-winners concert. This was good news for Miss Hill, but Yvonne and I were told that at the end of playing our piece, we should HOD HANDS while she curtsied and I bowed to the audience. Thirteen is an embarrassing age. In the event after playing, we both slid off the long piano bench, both gave a quick bow to the clapping audience and dashed off the stage. [Seventy years later I made use of this memory in the Scherzo chapter of my teen novel "Martin Ashworth Fourteen,"]

I passed the Silver Medal examination with 82 marks in December 1934. Miss Hill also entered me for various competitions run by the M.A.M. and other institutions at Stratford and London generally. I had to pass theory examinations as well and prepare for concerts at school and my parents' Methodist Church in the Romford Road, Manor Park. I collected the occasional competition 1st or 2nd medal, but more often a certificate of merit.

You may remember I was given "Solfegietto" to get my fingers running or dancing. I worked on this and the Chopin's Raindrops Prelude for a special trial MAM concert in May 1934. .Following this Russell Bonner, Director of studies, wrote me a personal letter inviting me to take part in the main

MAM Junior Students' Concert for all branches of the Academy on 7th June 1934. He added that they would put me down to play Bach's Solfeggietto, but there might not be time to play my second piece. I am sure Miss Hill was pleased.

At a WCHS concert on 5.7.1935 to celebrate the 250th anniversary of J.S.Bach, I took part in a school play/concert acting the part of the composer at the age of 10 and later, Emanuel a son. Then I played which Bach piece? You guessed rightly – Solfeggietto by C.P.E. Bach. I played it smoothly but fast, much to the disapproval of Miss Manley , the School's piano teacher. We had argued about this at rehearsal. She wanted it played much more slowly. She was a good pianist and played quite a lot during the evening. I may have been wrong, but if Russell Bonner liked my playing of Solfeggietto that was good enough for me.

Chapter 13 - Home Life

Brother Ken would have left our school at the end of my first year, July 1933. He took a job with a glove wholesaler in London as far as I can remember. He and I were interested in home chemical experiments as well as making fireworks. We used the shed at the bottom of our garden probably constructed by our Dad. Ken found he could buy chemicals cheaply somewhere near his City job. Then he persuaded me to try and sell them, with a small profit margin, to other members of my form at school. This went reasonably well for a short time until Russell found one item cheaper in his local shop. The scheme fizzled out shortly afterwards.

The Methodist Church on the Romford Road had quite a big effect on our parents' lives, specially I think in their early twenties. My father told me that they held educational classes to help those like himself, who left school early, There were Bates, Chesters and others of his age group in the 'Manor Park Fellowship'. My Dad once confided in me about his courtship of my mother. Daisy Bates. He told her that some of the other young men around had better prospects than himself. Then he proudly told me that Mum said to him, "But it's you I want." He also told me that she was the very best friend to have all his life. I was so pleased that he shared this with me.

Both Dad and Mum were members of the Church and took part in various activities such as jumble sales, socials, etc. Each year there was a special concert with local talent – including me when my fingers began to dance. In addition to the musical items, there was usually a sketch. I have an old programme of the Manor Park Fellowship Annual Concert of Feb. 13th 1936. It listed 16 items, one of them a sketch, 'Runaway Wives' performed by the Minerva Amateur Dramatic Society. The list of Artistes on the front cover included Master John Acton - Pianoforte and Mrs D Acton as one of the two accompanists. The tickets were sixpence or a shilling and programmes cost a penny. [A few years earlier the entry charge was by way of a 'silver collection': People used to collect the rare silver three-penny bits for the occasion.]

I played firstly a Beethoven Sonata in D Minor (Op.31 No.2) and then in the second half, Polichinella by Rachmaninoff. Another boy 'Artiste' was a singer. Master Alfred Rosenfield. I think it was in the second half that his pure treble voice tragically wavered and broke, something that happens at his age. I consoled him as best as I could. I noted this 'awful' happening in my diary. I was glad boy pianists did not have to face this hurdle.

Our Methodist Church was clearly doing a lot for the neighbourhood. On the back of the programme leaflet were advertisements for Sunday afternoon services with Guest Speakers and Popular Vocalists, Mutual Aid Sick Club, Fellowship Thrift and Loan Society and Mansfield House Coal Club. I also knew that there were the regular Morning and Evening Sunday services.

My father was in charge of the Sunday School for a time. Because of the distance from our home. I did not attend this Sunday School, although usually went on the large annual seaside outing. In fact I only attended a local Church Sunday School for a year. It made little impact on me.

My father kept up his friendship with the Chester brothers. I think it was Frank who sometimes came to our house to play chess with Dad. Guy who was quite well-off (stockbroker?) once invited our family to his mansion in Muswell Hill for a semi-social occasion. It might have been to mark the gift of a memorial window in his local church (not Manor Park then). I would have been 13 or 14. While we were there, Ken and one or two young people were invited to go to thee bottom of Guy's garden to see a cow that was kept there. I was left out of that party (too young?) but invited to go up to the first floor lounge and play their piano. I played 'The Hobby Horse' by Leo Livens that I had recently memorised. Pianists reading this might be interested to hear how I managed to learn to play descending chords fast, with alternate hands in triple time. I found it almost impossible to get away from one hand or the other dominating a simple duple rhythm. I finally solved the problem by plugging my ears as I played in triple time and gradually got used to it. Sorry for this diversion but it enabled me to play it sufficiently well to get by on this occasion.

Ken (17/18 ?)   Uncle Eddie   Myself (13/14 ?)

Brother Ken had joined the Scouts earlier, was very enthusiastic and soon made progress as a junior leader. He brought his pack or group home on one occasion, so that I could give them a film show, Harold Lloyd and cartoons, on my home Pathescope 9.5mm Projector. My Mum asked me about joining cubs or scouts, but I felt I needed the time for piano practice and homework.

As a family we started attending the Manor Park Methodist Church evening service when I was about twelve. We had a charismatic Welsh Minister who attracted a very large evening congregation. I think his surname was Beckwith, We sat in the gallery and enjoyed his powerful illustrations of the Gospel. Then we walked home by the back streets and gas light feeling that all was right with the world. How wrong I was, not realising what was happening in Germany.

Chapter 14 - Holidays at St Osyth Stone

I mentioned in 'My very earliest memories' that we had a trial beach hut holiday at St Osyth (Toosey) village beach. This inspired my Dad to investigate a proposed beach hut development at St Osyth Stone, immediately opposite Brightlingsea. It could be reached by train to Brightlingsea and row-boat ferry, or by car down a rough road from St Osyth to just beyond Point Clear. We tried both. Dad made a contract with the developer, a builder called Wade, to build the first wooden chalet on the sea wall facing out to the distant Mersea Island.

It was finished after a great deal of delays and queries in either 1932 or 1933 I think. It had two bunk bedrooms (i.e. sleeping four) with a kitchen/living room in front. At this stage there was no running water, electricity or gas. Cooking was by oil stove and there were oil lamps. The living space including a veranda, was all at the high sea wall level. Underneath was a garage and outside that, a small hut containing a chemical toilet. My Dad named it "ODTAA". Dad resisted explanation of the name, but finally told me it meant, "One damn thing after another!" but with no disrespect for Mr Wade. In fact he provided several amenities as time went by, including a free hard tennis court which gave immense fun to Ken and me.

There was also on the estate a Martello Tower, which was eventually let to a lady. She developed a Tower café and outside a separate small store for groceries and the essential supply of clean water, all of which had to be brought over from Brigghtlingsea by the primitive row-boat ferry. This lady, a widow, also organised social occasions in her historic Tower for Estate residents. As she had an upright piano I was sometimes asked to play. I composed a little piece in C Minor which I called 'The Tower Ghost' – a bit of fun which met with approval.

There were two or three ancient stones lying near the Martello Tower. I was quite young when I knelt down to re-tie my shoe-laces on one of these stones. I had almost finished when looking down at my other leg, I saw a long column of three deep red ants climbing up it and disappearing under the rim of my shorts !! I jerked up rapidly which was a signal for all the ants to start stinging. I yelled loudly. The irritation was unbearable. I ran fast back to Odtaa and luckily met my Dad near our garage. He rapidly stripped off my few clothes and was able to quickly wipe off the ants on to the garage floor. Then he wrapped me in an old coat and half-carried me up the outside staircase to the comfort of a bedroom. There Mum applied a sting-relief ointment she had in her medical store.

My niece Maureen and nephew Peter on the beach in front of the chalets in 1954
[As I could not find a thirties photo, I have had to use a 1954 snap to show the chalets and the beach.]

Primitive living ? Yes, but how wonderfully exciting for Ken and myself. The beach was rather stony with patches of sand. There were pools and a sort of stony mini- peninsula going a hundred feet or so out to sea from the shore, which got covered at high tide. We could fish from the sea wall outside our bungalow at high tide or from the end of the peninsula at low tide. Swimming was safe towards high tide. At low tide we could walk a hundred yards or more and pick out cockles which Mum liked. Ken and I bought or were given hand-lines. We dug worms for bait and soon became expert in catching mostly eels but some flat fish (flounders), which kept us in fishy meals. We reckoned to catch at least 200 eels during our summer holiday.

Two years or so later, Dad arranged for Wade to build a slightly bigger and more luxurious beach chalet almost next door to Odtaa. He called it "Dacton" based on Mum's name. This meant Odtaa could be let or used to house visitors such as family or friends.

As the estate developed and prospered, we would visit the neighbouring chalets and share out our surplus eels. When we had visitors who declared they did not fancy eels, Mum used to cook them, remove the skins and central bone before serving. As they enjoyed the delicious white fish, we would wait until they had finished, before revealing that they had eaten eels.

Behind our chalet was the Martello Tower already mentioned and the 'Saltings', marshy land mostly protected by sea walls and intersected with ditches and pools of mostly salt water. One could find edible mushrooms and also on the narrow foot-paths, basking adders. So we needed wellingtons if we wandered over the Saltings and kept wary eyes open for adders. I had to warn visitors with children more than once about this danger. We were only about a hundred yards away from Brightlingsea harbour which would be full of yachts, fishing boats and, of course, the two-penny row-boat ferry.

A year or so after buying Odtaa, my enterprising Dad bought a row-boat with a primitive mast and sail. It was mounted on a two-wheel trolley. We could push it round to the 'hard' on our side of the harbour and launch it ready for fun and advanced fishing expeditions. Ken and I developed rowing skills and also learnt to scull with one oar in a row-lock at the stern of the boat. This was a very useful skill. If we 'caught a crab' and lost an oar when rowing, we could scull with the remaining oar and quickly propel the boat to pick up the missing floating oar. We wore no life-belts or jackets. I had a quarter-mile swimming certificate from school, but at that stage I think Ken could only manage a few yards. We only occasionally used the sail. We kept an axe as well as the anchor and rope in the bow of the boat. We once went as far as Mersea Island on a fine day. It was good for fishing in the harbour, particularly if it coincided with the arrival of the shrimper boats. The seamen would cook the shrimps on board and throw residues into the water, attracting sea-gulls above and fish below the water-line.

On one occasion when I was 14 or 15, Mum agreed to go fishing with me in the boat, then anchored near the harbour. Ken would have been at work in London. I took fishing gear and anchored in what I thought was a good spot, in the middle of the fair-way out from the harbour.

My Mother in her Forties

We noticed a large commercial wherry or sailing ship coming out with the tide flow from Brightlingsea. I thought the ship would surely miss us, but NO ! It scraped our side and a seaman was swearing at us to get out of the way. I had been trying to pull up the anchor, but it was stuck. Mum was terrified – with reason. I could easily have jumped overboard and swum to the shore, but Mum could not. Our boat was now snagged on the hull of the ship and we were being tugged along out to sea. The seaman above us on the ship now had a long fending-off pole and repeatedly pushed it down onto our boar. Praise God we were suddenly pushed free of the big ship. I hastily pulled up the anchor (now freed) and rowed for the shore. Mum's face was white: perhaps mine was too or maybe flaming red with shame. I apologised very humbly. My Mum finally said, "I shall never go out again on a boat with you John." In retrospect I had made a grave error and risked my mother's life. I promised to be much more cautious in using the boat and sought her forgiveness, which she gave me. I think she must have played down my error in telling my Dad or else kept it from him. Was it my mother's prayers in the crisis that enabled the seaman to push our boat free?

Chapter 15 - Back to School and a teenage party

It is time to catch up with what has been happening at school. Towards the end of March1935, Grave told me he was holding a birthday party at his Ilford home on Saturday, 30th March. It would go on to very late on the Saturday evening. So his mother had agreed that a sleep-over to the Sunday morning could be arranged for myself and one other boy who lived at a distance from Ilford.

"Please will you come?" he asked. I hastily looked at my diary that I had started keeping. There were a few nearby musical dates – competition and a rehearsal, but I was free on the Saturday.

"Yes please. It sounds great but I must check with my mother, whom I hope will drop me and pick me up on the Sunday morning."

Next day I told Grave that I could definitely come. He was pleased and then nonchalantly dropped a bomb-shell by saying, "I have also invited a few of the girls from our form to come."

I was startled. This really was breaking down the School's (hidden) segregation policy – mixed classes but no social chatting, different playgrounds and mid-day lunch halls. "Gosh you're brave," I said.

"Don't worry. I have invited equal numbers of girls and boys," he said cheekily. I suspected then that he had probably been to other mixed parties and already knew some of the girls well enough to invite them.

On the special day, Mum dropped me at Grave's Ilford address in the early evening, complete with a small case containing pyjamas, towel, toothbrush and also a card and mini-present for Grave. About 7.30 p.m. the other guests arrived and we all assembled in a spacious lounge, ten or twelve of our form I would guess. I knew the boys, but who were that giggly cluster of girls in pretty party frocks at the far end of the room? They looked very different from the school girls, who we were used to seeing in their uniform gym slips.

Grave was a good host and proved an expert party organiser. He had an elder sister who had probably given him ideas. We were mostly still in two groups of the same sex. So he introduced a game which ensured each boy chatted up an individual girl. I cannot be positive but it was something like having two pots of numbered slips of paper coloured red (girls) or blue (boys). We all took one and had to find a match and say "Hello" and give our Christian names. Then we might have to play a simple game such as 'Paper, stone or scissors,' with our partner.

After that a return of our paper numbers to the pots and a fresh shuffle, with the proviso that we must find a different partner for the second round. Then there were games with balloons, drawing and acting clumps. I think the last was the most popular and caused much laughter. Then, of course, there would be a break for drinks, sandwiches and a slice of Grave's Birthday cake. We were all having a really good time, with no one left out. I admired Grave's careful planning and control of the evening. No wonder he was popular. We sang 'Happy Birthday' to him with gusto.

It was getting late when Grave astounded me and possibly most of us, by introducing his final game. It was not 'Postman's Knock' such as I had played way back with my girl cousins, Barbara(Babs) and Christine Stevens, who lived in Forest Gate. It was called 'Hyde Park Corner'.

"It is quite simple," said Grave placing an ordinary chair in the middle of the room. "I will demonstrate." He sat down on it and invited any girl who wished to do so, to come and sit sideways on his knee. Then he would give her a kiss. There was only a short pause before one girl came forward to sit down and receive a kiss. This was greeted with cheers, laughter and clapping.

"Now it's your turn Acton," said Grave smiling.

I blushed. I had been given no warning. This was a challenge. Would any girl fancy sitting on my knee and brave my specs in receiving a kiss? I wished I had taken them off, but I was quite short-sighted without them. I really had no choice, so I went forward and sat on the chair. Would any girl venture to come? I dared not look around but kept my eyes on the floor. There was a hush. Then I saw a pair of sandals coming into the focus of my eyes. It was my first partner of the evening coming shyly towards me, also with downcast eyes. As she got nearer she looked up briefly. I caught her eye, smiled and held out a hand. She had such a sweet serious face as she came alongside and sat sideways on my knee. I felt myself overwhelmed with emotion. I think we both completely forgot the watching crowd. I put my left arm round her waist and she moved her face closer to mine. I realised that she really wanted me to kiss her. So I gently kissed her cheek. This felt so good that, ignoring the crowd's cheers and clapping, I kissed her again. Then hastily (though reluctantly) I released her and we went our separate ways. After all it was only a party game played in full view of everyone. But for me it was such a profound experience that I never forgot it.

For weeks after I was teased about it. Apart from the odd smile on the rare occasion when we happened to pass one another on the stairways, we exchanged no further words. We both knew that at fourteen we would have no time for serious boy/girl friendships. I knew her name well but kept quiet about it at home. Nevertheless I was deeply indebted to Grave for giving me this 'growing up' experience. In my diary I wrote, "VERY GOOD" on the date.

Chapter 16 GCSE preparation: Miss Hinchley

School work progressed. Some subjects were dropped to enable concentration on those, in which we wanted to do well in the General School Certificate and Matriculation examinations. We would take these at the 15/16 year stage. I decided to drop Botany and History. We were given a new Form Teacher in Miss J.E.Hinchley, an English specialist. We still had Mr Swaine for Maths fortunately.

Ma Hinchley, as we privately called her, was also a strong character and did mother us to some extent. She gave practical advice to the girls, not to spoil their wonderful 'schoolgirl' complexions with cosmetic additions such as rouge and lipstick. We boys heartily agreed with that. She did add that some make-up could be suitable for some grown-ups. Then she started on us. She suggested that a lot of the hair lotions, gels or brilliantine, particularly the latter, were unattractive on boys. I thought Aldcroft looked uncomfortable. However, I could see the girls were enjoying this. I made a mental note to reduce my use of oily hair lotions.

Miss Hinchley loved books and taught us to treat them carefully. We were instructed to take them home and make brown paper covers to protect their valuable content. We had a lot of short essay writing homework. She also instituted form play-reading, Shakespeare and other dramatists. This was very popular and much enjoyed by Grave and me. I particularly liked taking the part of an old man, using the deepest voice I could manage.

In our second year with Miss Hinchley, she was asked to put on a short play at a school concert. Whether parents were invited I could not say. The play was "A Little Man" which I thought was by J B Priestly, but I am not sure. Strangely the hit pop tune of the day was "Little man you have had a busy day." I was given the 'Little Man' part. Grave and others also had acting and speaking roles. At least one scene had painted stage backgrounds, They mostly showed one side of a railway carriage. We took our seats carefully on the 'train benches' and said our lines. At the same time we had to simulate the train's motion by swaying gently in unison from side to side. I have forgotten the plot except that there was a fear that a travelling child might have a very infectious disease - its face was grubby and might be spotty. Acting as the brave 'Little Man,' I dramatically drew back the child's sleeve and said, "Look - as white as a banana !"

The actors got up quickly to look. Their reaction set the nearest stage background rocking. We panicked and tried to push it back up, but there was a knock-on effect on the adjacent stage scenery. Mayhem resulted with much back-stage activity. A great swell of laughter rose up from the hall. We were told by a grim-face Ma Hinchley to fall back and wait for the stage curtain to be lowered. Then we were led out to take a bow with applause and more laughter. In retrospect our play had accidentally become knock-about comedy, giving the greatest entertainment of the evening.

We apologised profusely to Miss Hinchley who realised that it was all accidental - and that perhaps the stage scenery should have been more securely fixed. Play time was over and we now had to concentrate on preparation for mocks and then the actual GSC and Matriculation exams.

Chapter 17 – Nazi virus appears

In 1936 – 1937 there was an interchange of Students with Cologne Secondary School. This statement is taken from the official programme for the Upper School Distribution of Prizes on 19th November 1937. I well remember the German boys coming, but had almost no contact since I studied French and not German. I think they all had to be part of some Hitler youth group. Our Jewish boys were uneasy at the time, but unprepared for what happened a little while after the departure of the German group.

I am unsure of the date but one morning break, I was late going down to the boys' playground. It was mostly empty. I heard noises and shouting coming from the direction of the coal store compound. I rushed down to it and found a crowd of boys watching a dreadful scene. Our Jewish boys had been secretly and suddenly rounded up by Seniors influenced by their German contacts. They had been forced to go into the coal storage shelter with nasty anti-Jewish taunts. Someone said that teachers had been alerted and would arrive shortly.

It was also time to get back to classes as the bell had sounded.

Later, Greenberg spoke calmly to me about his experience and said he was not physically hurt. I belive that Grave escaped the hunt - his Jewishness was less obvious than that of Greenberg and Goldberg.

I cannot remember any public denunciation of this shameful event in a school assembly. I think it was mostly hushed up. I doubt it got into the local paper. It was a politically anxious time for our nation.

Chapter 18 Home Life

My 1936 diary shows the death of King George V on 20th Janury followed by announcement of the new King Edward V111.

My Grandmother, Mrs Alice Hitchcock Acton

There is a mass of school dates, music dates, but then a heavily underlined note, 'Grandmother ill' on 22nd February 1936.   She died two days later. Grandad Acton was very sad and so was I. I did not know my paternal grandmother very well, but loved Grandad whom I saw more frequently. The funeral took place shortly afterwards.

My Dad and Mum's Silver Wedding was noted on 17th April 1936. The diary entries mostly peter out until a note of Mock Matric exams appear on several dates in June 1936.

On 20th July 1936 Mum took me to London for my final MAM examination. The next day I heard the result. I had passed with 72% but needed 80% or more to gain the coveted gold medal. So this was a serious failure in my progress. My sight reading had let me down with only 6 marks out of a possible 15. It was a very demanding examination. With scales requiring knowledge of major, minor and chromatic double thirds plus all kinds of arpeggios. Required music included a Beethoven Sonata, a Bach Fugue and a more modern piece. A huge amount of preparation was required. I invented my own system for remembering the fingering of the double thirds but it was not easy.

When the result was known, Miss Hill counselled me to take a break from working for a repeat attempt on the Gold Medal MAM exam. Instead I should consider working for a Diploma in due course. I also needed to learn a lot of new music to improve my sight reading.. The Summer holiday at our St Osyth Stone chalet was just about to start. That meant a long break from piano playing.

On return from the holiday I decided on working for a Performer's Diploma of the Royal Academy of Music, since this would avoid continual slogging away at the scales and arpeggios (not required). It would require a very much higher standard of playing more difficult piece, but this was my aim. Miss Hill helped me and that was probably when I began a preliminary start on Beethoven's great Appassionata Sonata. This was in the second book of Beethoven Sonatas which I had won as second prize in April 1935 at a London competition.

Meanwhile I spent most of my study time working for the GSE and Matriculation exams. I duly passed in 7 subjects with Matriculation exemption. Grave's name was missing from the results list. We had not seen him in school for a while which was a mystery. Greenberg and I thought that perhaps he was ill. But we had no information and we were all very busy on our various studies. We thought Grave would be bound to let us know if he had moved away or some tragedy had occurred. To my shame I was so centred on my own affairs that I let this matter slip.

Chapter 19 – Removal to Shenfield.

Towards the end of 1936 my Dad came up with another amazing project, to remove us from Manor Park to Shenfield on the North side of Brentwood, Essex. This was very exciting: a move of about twenty miles North of London to the Essex countryside. Our journey from Manor Park to St Osyth Stone used to take three hours in our Austin Seven. That journey time could be reduced by nearly an hour if we removed to Shenfield.

Dad had researched his project carefully. There was a very old property on the Shenfield to Chelmsford main road, which we passed every time we went to St Osyth. It was a picturesque timber-framed two storied old brick house, with an adjacent thatched wooden cottage. The house was named Elm Lodge, 108 Chelmsford Road. It had a very large garden compared with that of 12 Byron Avenue. There was a foot-path alongside it across fields to open country. AND it was very modestly priced at around £600 for the house and garden containing many excellent fruit trees, plus about £50 for the cottage inhabited by an old man with sitting tenant's rights. Dad had also checked that the walk from Elm Lodge to Shenfield Station, a railway junction with fast trains to London, was only about ten minutes.

Elm Lodge in recent times

Our family's first visit to see Elm Lodge was on 7th December 1936 but a closer inspection was deferred. My diary shows my concern about the abdication of Edward VIII on 10th December, which saddened me. Then came my sixteenth birthday on 12th December, mixed up with the accession of King George VI. We did some work on Elm Lodge garden on 23rd December just before the following Christmas festivities, family visits and presents at 12 Byron Avenue.

On 2nd and 3rd January 1937 we again visited Elm Lodge and this time met the tenant of Elm Cottage. Mr Dorin was a very pleasant old man who explained to me how he got his drinking water. Every morning he would take a small jug of water into our garden to 'prime' the pump on top of our well. Then he worked the pump handle up and down a few times to draw up enough water to fill a pail. Unlike Elm Lodge, he had no mains water or electricity supply, but had an outside toilet hut properly connected to a main sewer. He invited me inside to show me one or two old books such as an ancient atlas. I think later on he gave them to me. There was quite a strong smell of paraffin within.

20/10/2015

Elm Cottage –extended at far end since our time

We went on more visits, gardening and exploring Elm Lodge in greater detail. Dad had bought two architectural museums in effect. There was no furniture in the Lodge. Mum also said there was not a right angle anywhere! Beams abounded but in some bedrooms they twisted ominously downwards. The floor-boards were the very wide ancient type, but in a reasonable state. A very small entrance lobby led to a sitting room on either side. The right-hand one acted as a corridor to the toilet and kitchen and also housed the main staircase leading to three main bedrooms across the front, with a small attic and a bathroom at the back. There was also a small set of stairs tucked into one corner of the bedroom on the left. A small ground floor room at the back with a door to the garden, had some bottle glass in its window.

At the front driveway, there was a cherry tree, alongside a small lawn over-shadowed by a huge apple tree with a heavy drooping branch. There was a large triangular garden at the back with a ploughed field on one side. The footpath on the other side led to Hall Lane.

There were many fruit trees – two or three apple varieties, two pears, a large walnut tree and other delights such as a Medlar tree..

Footpath from Hall Lane leading to Elm Lodge

On 26th January 1937 I sat for the Civil Service Clerical Exam and passed it. Later I also took and passed the LCC Exam, but Dad assured me that the Civil Service was my best option. I should mention here that WHS teachers were very much against my dropping out of the sixth form and possible University education. A year earlier I made a diary note that Miss Hinchley had persuaded me to agree to go for a Higher Schools Examination. We had no phone but teachers probably wrote to my parents. Dad, who left school at fourteen, expressed the view that most of the senior Civil Servants were 'over-educated' (sic). However, he did give me the option of trying for higher education. He had reached the position of an Executive Officer in Customs and Excise. Certainly he was managing our family affairs, including a car, an Essex country home and holiday homes at St Osyth Stone, very well. My main interest was still piano studies, so I took his advice gladly. I would become a Cusoms and Excise Clerical Officer and this would give me two chances of taking the Executive Examination in due course.

Meanwhile our move to Shenfield was still progressing. I had several diary notes about packing stuff at home in preparation. We actually made our final move on Wednesday 24th March 1937'

Chapter 20 – Film audition

On Thursday we had our first post at Elm Lodge. Strangely it was for Master John Acton! It had been re-addressed from 12 Byron Avenue, Manor Park. School had stopped so I was home. Mum passed me the letter with eager curiosity. It was a very poor carbon copy letter dated 22nd March 1937 from a Second Floor address in Regent Street London signed by Wallace Orton. He stated that he had obtained my name and address from the Metropolitan Academy of Music and Dramatic Art. He was producing a film and needed young pianists for one sequence. I was invited to bring some music for an audition at a London address. Was it a hoax? The scrappy fourth or fifth carbon copy was barely legible and the audition date was for Thursday 25th March. While I was still wondering about it, Mum hurriedly read the letter. "Go for it John," she said. "Look - if you pass the audition, you will eventually appear in a film. I will take you to the rehearsals."

I could scarcely believe it, but we wrote off an acceptance and almost immediately I went up for an audition at some piano warehouse in London. This went all right. I was selected and sent some music, which I had to learn and know by memory when it came to filming. The first full rehearsal was at the Wigmore Hall on 2nd April. I found out we were a group of 7 boys and 7girls, some of whom I had previously met at various competitions in the London area. One of the boys, Lawrence Clark, a year or two younger than me, was also a pupil of Miss Hill. The pace of rehearsals quickened to one or more a week and further music arrived. Kennedy Russell, our musical director, had written arrangements of the William Tell Overture by Rossini and a pop song of the day titled, "When day is done (and shadows fall)." The first was exciting and well arranged but the second was less successful, so most of us thought.

My diary for the week beginning Monday 12th April 1937 shows me first at St Osyth Stone helping my Dad cement the frontage of Seagirt, another chalet he had bought. We went back to Elm Lodge that   evening, since I had further film rehearsals on Tuesday, Thursday and Saturday. On the Friday I had entered the Stratford Festival open piano solo competition for ages 15 – 16. I obtained the bronze medal (second place) and Sylvia Faust won the silver medal. I knew her slightly from previous contests and we were both in the team of juvenile pianists rehearsing for the film. Sorry if all this detail is boring, but I felt I ought to show the break-neck speed of working involved.

I was back to school on 21st April and was made a Monitor by the Headmaster on 27th April. I had to get special leave on 29th and 30th for the sound recording and then the final film shooting, both at Sound City Studios, Shepperton. We were promised a guinea a day and all expenses paid plus lunch, including an accompanying parent, for the days spent at the Shepperton studios. We learned that the film was called "Talking Feet" and featured a nine year old tap dancer, Hazel Ascot. Regretfully we did not get a chance to see her. We gathered that she might well become Britain's answer to the American girl star, Shirley Temple. Between our two group piano pieces, there would be a solo performance of Chopin's Polonaise in A Major by

Mark Hambourg, an ageing celebrity pianist. We saw him at a rehearsal and were able to secure his autograph.

Hazel Ascot

On Thursday 29th April 1937, Mum called me early, but I was already awake and washed, ready for the great adventure. Mum and I caught an early fast train to Liverpool Street: we were well used to the journey. But this time we went to the road leading out of the station to catch one of several taxis laid on by UK Films to take us all the way to Sound City, Shepperton Studios. Quite free, of course. We began to feel a little of the glamour of the Film Industry.

As our taxi was waved through the guarded gateway of Sound City, as it was called, we saw a number of large square detached concrete buildings. Each building or studio had red lamps fixed along it at intervals. Large notices placed along the road warned car drivers not to sound their horns, and to stop their engines instantly if the red lights showed. However, we passed through these safely and stopped before Studio Five. The production manager who had arranged our rehearsals, now known to us as Bob Jones, was there to greet us and show us to our dressing rooms, cloakrooms, etc., the dining hall and a lounge for the accompanying parents.

Then we were given our first glimpse of the real studio. We stepped into it through two heavily padded doors with an air space between. The chief things we noticed then were the walls. which were padded in a similar way to the doors, with the padding held in place by wire netting. There was part of a theatre built. On the stage and in fact every where, there was an army of carpenters working and making a fearful din. Scattered about in groups were both small and large arc lights all supported on separate metal stands. We looked upwards to the high ceiling and saw tiny figures perched on flimsy metal scaffolding, presumably attending to the arc lights up there. On the ground in front of us were literally hundreds of small, large and some very thick electric cables. One could not cross the floor without walking on some.

We then had a dress parade to make sure that our costumes fitted and were in order. The boys wore a black suit with white shirt, black tie and large white collar. The girls wore a frilly white frock with a large white bow adorning their hair. This inspection was done to a Director's satisfaction. Then we changed back to our ordinary clothes as the rest of the day would be spent on sound recording. This took place in a similar vast, but more empty hall.

After a preliminary rehearsal on fourteen Mini-Pianos, probably provide by the piano firm in an advertising contract, we had our first 'Take' or sound recording. A bell sounded. The padded entrance doors were shut. A red light gleamed in the roof. All the other red lights were switched on. A neon lighting sign, 'Silence,' also appeared just above the door. A man with a portable telephone signalled the sound engineers to say that we were ready. There came a low-pitched buzz from the telephone. A man stepped forward and said, "Sequence thirty-six, take one, sound track only-one, two, three," and clapped together two flat pieces of wood hinged together at one end. The moment after this our music conductor counted slightly faster from one to eight and then raised his baton.

After the suspense of this ritual, we pianists were rather nervous in our playing. It took two or three "takes" before we finally played to the best of our ability. After each "take", a rough recording of our work was played back and critically listened to by the Directors. In the end we were informed that the best portions of each recording would be cut out and spliced together. This would make one perfect and complete sound track.

This work took all day apart from the lunch break when we met up with our respective parents or guardians. Taxis took us back to London. I spotted no one I knew going back to Shenfield.

The next day, Friday, was scheduled for the actual filming. We were warned that we might also be needed on the Saturday to complete the job. Then came a minor shock. We each had to submit to an individual make-up session. It involved face paint, lip-stick and hands paint. The result made us look yellowish brown in ordinary daylight. I found wearing make-up very uncomfortable. I had also agreed to leave off my glasses for the filming. Then we were introduced to our positions on the big Hollywood style stage with five or six levels - see the 'still' photo below, courtesy of U.K. Films Ltd. I was on the right hand side, lowest level.

At the foot of the stage was the Scotch Kilties Band with a boyish conductor. They joined in only with the closing chords of our playing. In the body of the hall were about forty 'extras' (the audience) seated in a triangle arrangement: a full width at the front, but each succeeding line getting smaller. Thus a camera filming from the back could give the impression of a crowded hall.

On the set we had to endure the exhausting heat and light from the powerful arc lights, which were trained on us from every direction. The black and white filming like the sound recording, had a similar starting ritual. We listened to the clapper man and then Kennedy Russell counting one to eight, Then the recorded music and our simulated playing started together. We had to listen carefully to the recording to ensure an exact simulation for the cameras filming us from all directions, including overhead close-ups at times. This was the system used at the time. The sound we made this time was not recorded, only the filming. The sound and film tracks would be matched together in the cutting room. Owing to the glare and the heat we had to take frequent rests, so that the make-up ladies could powder our perspiring faces and do any other repairs necessary.

At the Friday lunch there was only pork on the menu which caused an irate protest from one of the parents, presumably of a strict Jewish faith. There was some sympathy for her and apologies from the management.

But I enjoyed the sausages. My mother was very interested in every detail of the recording and filming, Our make-up had been washed off before lunch, although it would be re-applied for the afternoon session. I told Mum about the roving cameras on the go all the time. I was very interested in the "Sky-Hi", a huge moveable crane with a mounted camera and high seats for the chief and assistant cine photographers and a producer. Compressed air from an electric generator was used by an engineer to control the valves of the hydraulic crane (so I was told). While we were playing, the crane camera would be moving around and taking individual close-ups or 'panning' general scenes. It was nerve-racking concentrating on playing our memorised music in exact timing with the recording, knowing that at any time the hovering cameras might choose one for a close-up.

We had completed our first piece, an arrangement of the Overture to William Tell by Rossini, which I thought was exciting and well done. We had also listened to Mark Hambourg play Chopin's Polonaise in A Major and duly clapped him on stage. I think most of us could play it and listened critically. Off stage we thought he played it a little too fast but kept this o ourselves. Our second piece, an arrangement of a pop song of the day, "When day is done (and shadows fall)," was less successful, we thought. Kennedy Russell had interlaced further themes which tended to obscure the perception of the main theme. We were told on the Friday that we were needed also on Saturday (a third day o filming).

On Saturday as a special treat, we were shown the film that we had made the previous day. We were very amused seeing ourselves playing on the screen. But there was more work to do, particularly on "When Day is Done." So we had to have make-up applied before final film shooting.

As a last treat we were assembled on stage for some group photos along with Kennedy Russell the Music Director and Arranger, seated at a mini-piano, Wallace Orton the Director on the right and Bob Jones the Production Manager on the left. I was in the top row, third boy from the left. Then for a short while as we said our farewells, we tried to get autographs of the three. film professionals and also of each other. The team's signatures are difficult to read. See below;-

Joyce Kenny? Sylvia A E Faust, Dolly Wolff, June Hitchcock, Ellen Rydell,? Joan Johnston?

Josephine Levy and Eric C.....? Lawrence Clark (pupil of Miss Hill), Edward R Gallagher? Eric Luck, Alvin F Lipsy?

Group photo on stage set - courtesy of U.K.Films Ltd

It was a happy conclusion to quite a strenuous time. We had each earned three guineas as professional junior pianists and enjoyed the experience. I was still rather shy with girls, despite Grave's efforts at his party. I would have liked to chat more with Sylvia Faust but we were sent off to the dressing rooms fairly quickly to change and prepare for home.

Within a week of the filming I wrote an account for the WHS Heronian magazine. This helped a lot in my getting correct details of the filming procedures at Shepperton in 1937.

Chapter 21 - Return to norm al life

Following the end of the Easter holiday, I travelled back from Elm Lodge to school for my final term at WHS on 21st April 1937. I used a coach service this time. The next day was Dad's 49th birthday and I gave him Coronation Chocolates (probably helped by Mum). Then came film shooting as already described.

On 5th May I was notified that I had passed the Civil Service Clerical exam. My position was 414th out of 2,ooo successful – very mediocre although there were 7,300 entrants. I think the St George's correspondence course I took had failed in explaining the Arithmetic short cuts used, as I scored only 15 out of 100! Whereas in Mathematics I scored 194 out of 200. Dad gave me £1 for persistence. In the School sports day on 8th May, I was delighted to cheer my friend Russell for achieving Victor Ludorum by a good margin.

The coronation of George VI was high-lighted on 12th May. I had a Civil Service medical with our local Dr Gibson, who was very nice and suggested I might become Chancellor of the Exchequer one day. We now went more frequently to our sea-side bungalow/chalet from Elm Lodge. Om Sunday 30th May I noted that I had caught two eels and played tennis with Ken. The next day I was so pleased that we were able to move my beloved Nan into Elm Cottage.

Church-going. Almost nil once we had removed to Elm Lodge at Shenfield. We were away a lot at St Osyth Stone at weekends, and would come home late on a Sunday evening. I can remember we visited the Brentwood Methodist Church once, but it seemed very different to the Manor Park one. Further my Dad was incensed that his and Mum's membership at Manor Park, had been transferred to Brentwood Methodist without his agreement. I really missed those evening services listening to the Rev. Beckwith (if I have his name correct). I did suggest trying the Brentwood Methodist again but the subject got dropped. And our Church-going fell into disuse. I was also near to starting my Civil Servie career plus keeping up my piano studies with Miss Hill.

Chapter 22 - Entry to H.M.Customs and Excise.

On Monday 14th June I went up with Dad by rail to Liverpool Street. We caught the underground to Mark Lane and walked through the famous Billingsgate fish market to the Custom House in Lower Thames Street. After consultation I was assigned to the ground floor Registry. I met the Superintendent , Mr Phythian (spelling a guess), who was friendly and handed me over to an older man to teach me my job. It was basically recording the movement of files and their sometimes voluminous and heavy attached papers (called FP) from one office to anther. We had to read the final enclosure of each file to find out where it was intended to go, write a direction on the outer cover, record the details in our desk register, and then place the file bundle in the appropriate slot in a rack above our desk. The files were tied up with thin white tape. A very old file might still be tied up with the famous bureaucratic red tape. As we got expert we could get to throw (if Mr Phythian was not watching) the file bundle into the correct slot, without getting out of our seat. The staff were either youngsters like myself, or really old ex-service men who had endured the horrors of the Great War. There was one man with only one arm who was well-liked. They sometimes talked about their experiences, the dread of having to go 'over the top'. But they avoided shocking us with awful details. Unlike school there was no ban on chatting so long as we got our work done. There was some friendly chaffing about our youth and inexperience. One man said he had seen a report by a Waterguard Officer, who wrote, " I climbed up the Jacob's ladder on the side of the fishing boat I had to search. When I reached the top I was hit with a belaying pin! This aroused my suspicions!" I think this was a classic Customs' joke and we duly laughed.

I was paid £85 per annum, working 9 to 4 or 10 to 5 with lunch 1-2 p.m., five and a half days a week except occasionally I might be required to stop Saturday afternoon on my own. This was in case there was an urgent request for a file from one of the Executive Sections. I was allowed 24 days annual leave. Dinners in the Customs' Luncheon Club would cost 5/- a week. The railway season ticket would cost £5:10s: and 6d for three months. Dad agreed I could have four shillings a week pocket money and suggested I should try and save half in a P.O. Savings Bank. The remainder probably went to Mum for house-keeping.

I should add that all new appointments were on probation, maybe for a year, and subject to efficiency reports before 'Establishment' would be granted. I apologise for all these details, but they may interest some.

On Wednesday, 30th June, I stood in line with others to receive my first Civil Service pay in cash,, £3 :18:6 ½.

The next day, 1st July 1937 in the evening, I went with my mother to the 'Trade' showing of Talking Feet. It was held in the West End at the Phoenix Theatre. The Upper Circle seats were C 22 and 23 - I still have the stubs. At one point I was awe-struck when my close-up filled the whole of the cinema screen. "Is that really me?" I asked her. "Yes dear," she whispered back.

It was classed as a B Movie but had good write-ups

Back at the Customs and Excise registry, I told one or two of my young fellow-workers about my playing in a B Movie. They did not believe me. I scarcely believed it myself. Meanwhile shortened week-ends continued at the 'bungalow' as we called it. Ken had a holiday from his work in the City and spent it at the bungalow with cousin Victor.

On 13th July I had a letter from the Film Company asking whether I could make some personal appearances with the showings of the Talking Feet film. It was not practicable for me - so goodbye to all that.

Generally I was very happy with life. I enjoyed the beginning of independence that a reasonably paid job in the Customs gave me. There was an early prospect of moving to a more interesting job in one of the Executive Sections, such as where my Dad worked. I tried a City night class to work for the Executive exam but found it unsuitable so started on a correspondence course. Miss Hill was very accommodating in fixing times and places of my piano lessons, e.g. a studio close to Ilford Station.
Ken and I had friends (the Slaughters) in Hutton Mount who would invite us over to play tennis, which was good. There are also references to billiards and Monopoly in my diary.

We celebrated Ken's Twenty First Birthday at Elm Lodge on Tuesday 17th August 1937.I detailed all the presents and cost if known! An umbrella 16/11 from me, a watch £5 from Dad,, clothes from Mum, a suitcase from Auntie Vi and Uncle Harold, fountain pen from Nan, gold cuff-links from Uncle Ernie, two telegrams and sixteen letters (presumably enclosing cards and maybe postal orders?). There were so many people there that Ken was seated half-way up the stairs at Elm Lodge.

Mum had her birthday on Sunday 29th August at the bungalow. Ken gave Mum a lovely pair of gloves - he was presumably working for a glove wholesaler at that time. I gave her half of a choc. box and ten cigarettes! At work on Wednesday I noted I had 50 BFs to do, i.e. I had to locate from store and send up to the Sections, fifty files that were due to be 'brought forward' for attention. But I was looking forward to my first official annual leave - two weeks staring on Monday 27th September, spent partly at the bungalow and partly at home. On Sunday 3rd October Ken and I had a record haul of fish,, 19 flounders and 6 eels, probably caught in the harbour following the arrival of the Shrimpers with their catch. Back home on Tuesday 5th October, I bought myself a new grey flannel suit from the Houndsditch Warehouse and treated Mum to see "Talking Feet" at the Astoria Cinema. [Thereafter I did not see the film again for 77 years].

My diary continued with mostly routine notes until my Seventeenth Birthday on 12th December 1937. This is simply noted " * My Birthday * " with no mention of presents, although I am sure there were some. There was also little mention of Christmas. A financial note at the back revealed that I had taken my first attempt at the Executive Officers exam and had failed to secure a place. My Dad, however, had given me a £1 'for persistence'.

I think that is perhaps a suitable note with which to end this attempt to describe my first seventeen years of life. Whether it was school work or piano-playing, there were always others more brilliant. But I got by with persistence, making the best of what I could do. I regret that I was so self-centred that I neglected to enquire further as to what happened to my friend Grave. I also regretted losing that contact with the Methodist Church in Manor Park. I owe a great debt to my Mum, Dad and brother Ken for their love, care and guidance in my growing stages.

[Continued in Part 3 – Epilogue 1939 to 2015]

MY LIFE STORY   PART THREE

Epilogue – 1939 to 2015

Chapter 23 – War declared

Despite appeasement efforts by Neville Chamberlain, a war to stop Hitler's grandiose expansion plans and vile treatment of Jewish and other minorities seemed inevitable. Nevertheless I was stunned when War against Germany was actually declared on Sunday 3rd September 1939. Standing with my Dad under the cherry tree at the gate to Elm Lodge, I said, "How can grown men be so stupid? It's MAD." My Dad agreed, sadly.

An immediate response from brother Ken and two or more of his friends in their local Amateur Radio Club, was to quit their jobs and join the Armed Services as radio operators.

I was still working in the Custom House in London. I had taken my second E.O. exam earlier but was below the successful line. However, with the onset of war the intake was extended and thus I scraped by (once again) to take up an Executive Officer job in Customs on 19.12.1939. My Dad was also upgraded to temporary HEO.

I met another new young EO in the Custom House called Alan Mason, with a home in Leigh-on-Sea. We soon became firm friends. We usually had lunch together and enjoyed short walks round the City and also the banks of the Thames at low tide. When he enlisted in the Army some time in !940 (I believe), we both agreed to keep in touch throughout the War, and so we did.

Meanwhile, I continued with commuting to the Office, piano lessons and tennis at the Brentwood Club section of the Essex Cricket Club. I met a lot of friendly youngsters there, including girls. One girl in particular I dated, but the relationship fizzled out after a while. I remember once sheltering in a wide ditch at the tennis club in September 1940, while overhead we saw Spitfires and Messerschmitts shooting at one another in furious dog-fights. A battling pair of fighters came down very low, possibly 200 or so feet above us. We could hear the rattle of machine gun-fire with spent cartridges falling to the ground. It was an awesome close-up of a critical stage in what became known as the Battle of Britain.

While playing tennis in 1940 I fell awkwardly and badly injured my left knee. It was an injury that was never properly diagnosed until six months later by a West End Osteopath, Dr Wareing. The inner ligament had jerked out of place. In a dramatic session after massage with olive oil, Dr Wareing gave a sudden wrench on my knee. There was an audible click as the ligament was pushed back into its correct slot. For the first time since my fall, I could bend my left leg properly. I was instructed to take off the bandage and massage daily with olive oil.

Chapter 24 – RAF service

I was still massaging my knee when I was called up into the RAF on 25.6.41 to train as a Wireless Mechanic.

Brother Ken   **Myself**

Following kitting out with uniform at a small aerodrome, Stapleford Tawney in Essex, I was due to be posted up North to Padgate for initial training. I had one Sunday free in Essex and decided to take a bus into Romford. There I discovered a Methodist Church with a morning service just beginning. I went in. The hymns were familiar and reminded me of Manor Park. The sermon was based on Luke's story of Simon, a Pharisee, who invited Jesus to a dinner at his house, but neglected to give him the customary greetings reserved for more honoured guests. A fallen woman was also there, weeping and wetting Jesus' feet with her tears. She used her hair to dry them and then anointed them with expensive perfume. Jesus compared her welcome with that of Simon and rebuked him saying, among other things, "You gave me no kiss." Then the Minister challenged us on our treatment of

Jesus. Might a day come when Jesus might say to us, "You gave me no kiss." I must apologise for this somewhat crude summary of the story, but it had a big impact on me. From then on I attempted to find out more about this Jesus. whom I had neglected for so long.

I had a tough two weeks at Padgate (near Warrington) square-bashing in my new boots. It was tough on my feet and my weak left knee which swelled a little. I used my private bottle of olive oil for massage every night and just avoided having to go sick. We had to march through Warrington carrying our heavy kit-bags before catching a train to London. A few days in billets in Portman Square and then transfer to civilian billets close to Battersea Polytechnic for technical training. This was heaven after Padgate. The course was amazingly comprehensive, including metal working, soldering, theoretical magnetism and electricity and radio reception and transmission. We had free time most evenings and Sunday. I was able to get some social contacts at a local chapel which ran a Junior Church on Sunday mornings. After tests in which I did well, I with four or five others were selected for teacher training. We were eventually given the rank of Temporary Wireless Mechanic Corporal and posted to Cranwell. There we completed our training on the specialised equipment used in RAF aircraft and ground Wireless stations.

I was soon given my own class-room teaching about wireless receivers as used in the RAF. It was a real privilege to be at Cranwell. We worked hard six days a week but most of Sunday was usually free. They had a music society which met weekly, gramophone recitals one week and live music the next. They also had a decent grand piano. Corporal Peter Sallis (later famous for acting as Clegg in the 'Last of the Summer Wine') was secretary. I soon got to know this witty character. I was often invited to play piano solos and also to be an accompanist for the many amateur musicians in the ranks of the RAF. One such was Cpl Ronald Huddy, a skilled violinist. We were able to practise for hours together on V and P Sonatas by Beethoven, Mozart etc. I had never previously enjoyed such exciting music. We sometimes missed our Sunday lunch so as to get in a little more practice. We became close friends.

We also had professional musicians visit to entertain us and I got to know the very talented pianist Denis Matthews (then with the rank of a corporal). I once had to turn the pages for him when he played in a piano quintet with Sgt Griller and his boys. They were in fact the internationally famous Griller String Quartet. Sgt Griller made a few opening remarks to a crowded hall, with Officers in the front row and other ranks seated behind. He said, "The other week, we played at an Officers' Mess of an unnamed airfield. As we were playing an energetic Allegro, I became aware of someone tapping me on my back. I did my professional best to carry on with the music approaching a fortissimo. Then I heard a voice saying close to my ear, "I say old chap. Could you play less loudly? We cannot hear ourselves talking!" The whole room exploded with laughter. There might have been the odd red face in the front row.

As mentioned above, I was faced with accompanying all manner of singers and instrument players, usually without rehearsal. So many that my weak sight-reading began to improve ready for my Diploma attempt after the War ended. I am ashamed to mention that in addition to these musical delights, we also had use of an indoor swimming pool.

Chapter 25

Brother Ken in the Army had progressed to Sergeant. In June 1942 he became engaged to Mary Haynes of Honiton. On 3rd December of the same year he, married her in the local Honiton C of E Church. I was very privileged to be his Best Man. Mary's mother, Mrs Haynes, was a widow and very charming. She got on well with my Mum and Dad. Ken and Mary were well suited and obviously deeply in love. So we were all delighted, even though it was only a short break from the stress of War for Ken.

Ken's marriage to Mary Haynes at Honiton, Devon

Back at Cranwell during 1943 Ron Huddy and I kept busy playing V and P sonatas plus my solos and accompaniments at the Music Society. Ron and I were also invited a couple of times to give concerts at the Sleaford Music Society. At the swimming pool I learned to dive off the swinging trapeze and swim two continuous lengths under water. In November 11943 I had to go sick with Impetigo. This may well have upset one of a number of overseas postings I had which never took place..

On 19.2.1944 I began a series of postings to active service aerodromes that led to Selsey, South of Chichester, where I witnessed the first of Hitler's 'Doodle-Bugs' to arrive. We were preparing to take part in Eisenhower's Tactical Air Force. My immediate job was to equip a 30cwt van with wireless mechanic tools. Then use them (with a couple of LACs) to maintain and repair wireless equipment in Spitfires and Hurricanes. These planes were adapted to carry cameras to help in reconnaissance and photograph D Day landings. [This all happened while, unbeknown to me, brother Ken was with the allied invading army on D Day plus three.] We were all inoculated ready for overseas service when there was a sudden check.

An inspection from a high ranking Officer one day, highly praised our well prepared mobile workshops, signals, instruments, fitters, engineering, etc. Then he said, "These vans are just what I need at ---------- (some place in France). I must have them urgently." We were all devastated. We had lost our vans, but we were disbanded and sent off to various places.

Happy group of fellow mechanics at Blackbushe Aerodrome

[I am on the left of the top row. Third from the left is Ken (Basher) Howe, one of my chums who was later posted to Japan and wrote to me from Hiroshima. He died quite a few years ago. I remained in touch with his family.]

I went off to Blackbushe in Surrey, Ruislip in London and then to Bletchley where I worked eight hour shifts maintaining the giant transmitters and receivers of this important communication hub for the war effort. We had no idea of the secret decoding work being done in various huts on the site. But we presumed there must be a number of people involved in deciphering the teleprinted tapes. On the night shift, as Corporal with just two or three men, I was in sole charge of keeping the transmitters, receivers and teleprinters working.

[I earned a Bletchley badge for my short service. But I was dismayed to see only the Mansion remaining with all the extensions to house the giant transmitting valves, and other signals gear completely gone, when I visited a few years ago.]

Brother Ken was demobbed on 17.12.1945 after the arduous and heroic invasion of France. He told me he had at least two drivers shot alongside him while travelling. He also nearly lost his life from asphyxiation in the back of his signals van. Fortunately he was pulled out and revived just in time. When I saw him he looked really fit. He said he had survived with three narrow squeaks. He was rejoicing to be safely home with Mary and their baby daughter Maureen, my niece, born on 15.4.1944.

Chapter 26 – Demob

My service at Bletchley ended in June 1946. I was finally demobbed on 22.6.1946. In my five years in the RAF I had been given five or six overseas postings and three embarkation leaves, but I never left England. Two postings failed because of my going sick with infections (Impetigo and Scabies). The others failed due to the 'exigencies of war' or plain administrative inefficiency. I was really embarrassed and annoyed when my third embarkation leave came to naught. But now I was FREE with 56 days of glorious leave before going back to my waiting job in Customs and Excise.

Back home in my Demob Suit (courtesy of the RAF), I sent off for the LRAM Performer's Prospectus. After a short break I started piano practice in earnest - nothing less than four or more hours a day would be needed to master and memorise the forty minutes performer's programme by December, even though I had been working on some pieces such as the Beethoven Appassionata for years. At home I now had an old Ibach Boudoir Grand that I bought locally for £75 in April 1945. It made a huge difference to my ability to master difficult finger work. I renewed lessons with Miss Hill. Nearer the time of the examination she arranged three or four venues where I could get concert playing experience. One was at the Kingsway Hall in London where the Minister, Rev. Donald Soper,(well-known for his open-air debates on Tower Hill) also played a clever comic piano piece.

My mother came with me to the Royal Academy of Music for the performance exam on 19.12.46. It was bitterly cold and when I started on the Bach prelude, I fumbled and begged to be allowed to warm my hands at the open fire. The two elderly examiners were sympathetic and agreed. After that all went reasonably well. The next day I sat for the paperwork tests. After Christmas I heard that I had passed on practical performance but was a mark or two short on one of the theory papers. I had two more chances of sitting the paperwork tests within a year and pass all three to gain the coveted diploma. I was reminded of my struggles to pass the EO exam.

Office work continued happily now at City Gate House, Finsbury Square. I met up with Alan Mason who suggested a short hiking Youth Hostel holiday in the Peak District. He had also promised such a holiday to his sister when the war was over. He asked me, "Would that be all right with you? If so I will organise it." (I dimly remembered my school friend Grave asking me a somewhat similar question.) I gratefully accepted his kind offer. So it was on 25.3.1947 that I first met Doreen Mason with her brother at St Pancras Station in time to catch the 8.55 a.m. train to Sheffield. She was quiet, pretty and natural. I was impressed.

Chapter 27 – YHA holiday.

During the train journey I explained that I was preparing for my second attempt on the LRAM paperwork. I needed to work on a four part harmony exercise. They kindly kept quiet but probably thought me odd. At one point Doreen offered me a pear. I felt I should accept it and started to eat it . Then I was horrified to find later that they were sharing the only other pear they had. This incident became a family joke.

Our five days went very well thanks to Alan's careful planning. The Peak scenery was great. We went across

Mam Tor in mist and clambered down steep slopes carefully holding hands for safety (Alan's instructions). One or two evenings in a hostel, I ventured to play some of my classic piano pieces. By the third day I had completely lost my heart to Doreen. She was highly intelligent like her brother, natural and beautiful. I dared not say anything to Alan, who had told me Doreen ought to go on to University. When we got home, I now had two aims. The first was to get to know Doreen better; the second was to keep up my music theory studies,

In September 1946 I had bought my first car, a 1933 sports SS9 two-seater for £200. It was a very poor bargain and often broke down. Reasonable second hand cars were difficult to find at that time. I had joined Ken's old Hockey Club and was using the car to go to various hockey matches in Essex, sometimes giving a lift to another player.

So it was in this car that I first drove down to 39 Marguerite Drive, Leigh-on-Sea to see Doreen. Alan was surprised but accepted my interest. I had a very warm welcome from Doreen's parents. The car did not behave well. The engine tended to stall, probably with a choked carburettor. It was very embarrassing. On one occasion, not the first, I was fiddling with it for hours. I took Doreen out in the car on local trips. On 19th April 1947 I noted, 'Visited Southend Pier with Doreen.'

I discovered that she worked in a Bank of England office in Finsbury Circus, which was not far from my Customs office in Citygate House, Finsbury Square. We planned to meet secretly in the lunch hour and perhaps have a quick snack in a nearby café. This was great fun and worked well for a few times. My office people never found out, but two or three of Doreen's office colleagues spotted us and I had to be formally introduced.

Chapter 28 – Doreen challenges my faith.

Visits to Leigh-on- Sea continued. Doreen took me to her Baptist Church at the top of her road for the Sunday morning service. The Minister was the Rev. John Pritchard, who gave eloquent penetrating sermons in the style of the Manor Park Methodist preacher of my early teen years. Doreen and I had serious talks about what we believed. Her faith had been helped by her involvement in the local Girls Crusaders Union group. She said I needed to commit my life to Jesus before she could consider deepening our relationship.

I recalled that early sermon from the Romford Methodist preacher about Jesus saying to Simon, "You gave me no kiss." Apart from odd occasions, I had neglected Him in favour of progress at work or in piano music. Now I was striving and praying for God to help me believe in the reality of Jesus, and not just because I wanted to win the love of Doreen. I told her that I appreciated what she had said. I was trying hard to gain a faith like hers. On 26th April I took her to see a play in London called "Candida". That same evening I played (by invitation) at a second concert in the Kingsway Hall (Dohnanyi, Leo Livens and Chopin). I think my Dad separately crept in to hear my performance, so as not to intrude on me and my girl.

On a couple of restless nights in late April or May, I had strange experiences of an inner voice saying to me that "Jesus is real. Jesus is real." Nothing will ever shake me from this certainty or the need to do something about it.

On 3rd May 1947 I was a contestant at the Wanstead Open Chopin competition. I won it playing the last movement of the Third Chopin Sonata in B Minor, the most difficult Chopin I had ever mastered The competition was closely contested and the top two contestants each had to play a repeat section. I was declared the winner by a very small margin. I came out of the hall elated, started my car and drove all the way to Marguerite Drive where I had been invited to stop the night. Alan was taking part that evening in a local Musical called Rose Marie. The next day, Sunday, I took Doreen for a drive after lunch. I told her of my desire to commit my life to Jesus and would she marry me. She expressed her delight but cautiously said she needed a little more time to consider it.

Chapter 29 – Commitment and Engagement

On another Sunday I sought an interview with John Pritchard and he led me in a prayer of commitment. Doreen supported me and I was deeply moved. On Sunday 18th May 1947 Doreen promised to marry me. At her Mum's suggestion, I went to see her Dad in the front parlour and formally asked his permission to marry his daughter. He shyly agreed - I think he was as embarrassed as I was. So we were now engaged. I had to think about getting Doreen a suitable ring and working out a wedding date. It was also Alan's birthday but I don't think he was around. When I did see him , strangely enough I remember it was at Liverpool Street Station. He rushed over and gave me a wonderful brotherly greeting. "I am so glad you are now part of our family. If there is anything I can do for you, just ask me," he said. Then came meetings with Doreen's elder brother Charlie and his wife Dorothy and most importantly of all, my Mum and Dad. It took a few days to choose and buy the engagement ring. I see from my diary that the 28th May was treated as our official engagement day with Doreen wearing the ring.

Photo taken by Ken's wife Mary

It was probably just before Doreen came for a weekend at Elm Lodge. My Mum immediately embraced her in welcome with my Dad a little less demonstrative. There were also congratulations coming in from Ken and Mary at Honiton, Devon. Mary was expecting her second child. Peter John Acton duly arrived on 20th June 1947.

Our wedding plans moved swiftly ahead . I sold my car for a low price. I knew I could not afford a car and marriage at this stage   We fixed the date of 20th September 1947 for our wedding at the Leigh Road Baptist Church.

Wedding Day photo taken by Uncle Eddie Bonner

Family and friends Wedding group in garden at Leigh Road Baptist Church

But where we should live remained a tricky problem. My Dad and Mum generously solved it for us by offering to let us use two or three rooms at Elm Lodge. We had the West top bedroom and attic, with the little staircase leading down to a small store room at the back of the house. In this back room we installed a gas cooker and a small ceramic sink with only a pail for a drain. I provided the running water by dashing from our back door to Mum's kitchen with a jug. Dad worked it all out and we thought it was heavenly. Of course I still had my grand piano in the front room under our bedroom.

Doreen resigned from the Bank of England two or three weeks in advance of the wedding. My mother helped her with getting needed household items. We sent off lots of invitations and received many gifts. We also booked our honeymoon, two weeks at a modest hotel in Ambleside in the Lake District. It all happened so quickly, the wedding, friends and family photos, reception, speeches (including that of Best Man Ken), cards and presents, one night in a London Hotel and rail journey to Ambleside. The late September weather was unusually fine. We ranged freely over the glorious countryside with its hills and lakes.

Bliss - exploring the Lake District on our Honeymoon

We thanked God morning and evening for His gracious goodness to us. It was a taste of Heaven even if we were a little hungry at times due to food rationing.

Chapter 30 - Our first home and activities.

Then we came home to Elm Lodge and another warm welcome. My Mum cooked us a couple of meals. Then she said, "It's up to you now to get all your own meals." Doreen was not very experienced in cooking, but she quickly acquired a smll library of recipes and cook books. When I came home from work, I would see her com e staggering out of our kitchen with a load of books, before bringing in the meal. I enjoyed my office work but going home to Doreen every evening was such a huge delight. Could life get any better ? We found it could.

Because of Doreen's GCU contacts, I had a visit one evening from J.M.Vellacott, the leader of the local boys' **Crusader Class.** He badly wanted a pianist to play the hymns and choruses in the Sunday afternoon class at Brentwood School, leaving him free to give the lessons, etc. He was charming and I readily agreed. Little did I know then Crusaders would become one of the special things I should do for the Lord. I stayed for some 38 years at Brentwood Crusaders, eventually becoming the senior leader in charge of the Class.

Brentwood Crusaders Whitsun Camp at Danbury 1972

I wish I could safely remember all the names although the faces are familiar. Top row from the left I think there is Keith Ison (now an OBE) followed by naughty Paul Wickens holding a bucket over someone. Next to that someone to the left I think is Rowan Callick (now an OBE) and left again is Philip Bender. Also in that row are Alan Hayman (missionary and TV producer) and wearing glasses, David Ison (now Dean of St Paul's). In the third line down, second from left is my a stalwart Scottish co-leader, Alan Campbell, then Kenneth Horsnell, a friend of mine who acted as 'Padre' for this camp.

I am still in touch with some of my fellow leaders and old boys to-day. I look up with awe at a number who have achieved and continue to achieve so much in their service for the Lord.

CSCU – Customs Branch

I must go back now to my early day of marriage. At work I enquired whether there was a Christian Union. I discovered that pre-War there had been a Customs branch of the Civil Service Christian Union. Doreen had a Christian friend working in Customs,, Margaret Wilkinson. She and two or three others agreed to help if I could restart the CSCU Customs branch. After contact with central CSCU, I wrote formally to our Head Office seeking the necessary permission to start and to put up a Notice. This was speedily given and we started a half an hour weekly lunch-time meeting in the nearby Billingsgate Mission Hall that had been established for the fish porters and market traders. It was agreed that I should be secretary and invite speakers one week, while members themselves would undertake a Bible study alternate weeks. Later we also had a weekly prayer meeting. These meetings continued, sometimes at different venues and were still being held when I retired at the end of 1980.

Start of our own family

A visit by Doreen to our local doctor on 28.11.47 confirmed that she was pregnant. I felt sure it would be a boy. We praised the Lord for His goodness to us. We had been visiting the local Churches and finally settled on Brentwood Baptist Church, where we were made very welcome.

For my Birthday on 12th December 1947, Doreen gave me a Schofield Bible which I found interesting. Following Christmas festivities at Elm Lodge, we received an invitation to Doreen's brother Alan's wedding to Kip Redman at Leeds on 12.3.48. I was honoured to be his Best Man. Kip's father was a Methodist Minister and there were other Methodist Clerics there: at least two of them commenced their speech by saying, "Unaccustomed as I am to public speaking ...." which caused some amusement.

Coming home from work on 8th May 1948 I saw Doreen waiting for me at the door waving a letter. I saw it was from the Royal Academy of Music. I rapidly opened it to find that I had finally passed the LRAM paperwork by a very small margin. As I kissed her thankfully, I realised I had just scraped through on my last chance to gain the Performer's Diploma. My Mum was so pleased. If I had been much younger, I am sure my Dad would have given me another £1 for persistence.

Chapter 31 - Start of family.

On First July 1948 baby Thomas Alan Acton arrived. He weighed 8lb and 11 oz which meant a difficult time for dear Doreen. They came home to Elm Lodge on 14.7.48. Doreen had various baby management books. We wrestled with strictly disciplined feeding time schedules as against 'feeding on demand'. The latter finally won.

Thomas (about two years) and I outside Elm Cottage

We enjoyed a brief visit from Ken and Mary and Doreen's Mum during this period. My Mum loved giving Thomas a 4 o'clock cuddle no matter what schedule he was on.

I must now begin to finish this detailed history with just a few dates :-

1.12.48 Doreen, I and Thomas moved to Elm Cottage (Dad's gift). Shortly after this Dad and Mum sold Elm Lodge to a Doctor and moved to Aventine on the Martello

Tower estate. After a few months they moved first to St Osyth and then to central Clacton, 41 Henges Road.

8.8.49 Doreen and I were baptised by full immersion ,at Brentwood Baptist Church. Later we did spells as deacons, etc., and held a weekly home Bible Study group.

2.1.50 I was promoted to HEO in Customs

27.7.50 Alice Mary Acton (our second child) was born

14.5.52 Building plans for a four bedroom detached house and garage in Holmwood Avenue, Shenfield, were approved (My design redrawn by an architect for the Council)). We named it 'Limpsfield' as the Avenue had not yet been assigned numbers. We loved it when people asked us whether we had a connection with Limpsfield, Surrey. We would answer, "No. It is the name of a hymn tune - We have heard a glorious sound, Jesus saves."

17.6.52 Jonathan Ralph Acton (our third child) was born.

2.1.53 Completion of building on our plot 50 by 200 feet of ploughed field. We moved in shortly afterwards.

23.2.54 Billy Graham started his London campaign. I went and was impressed by the evident blessing. I later became a Counsellor at all the subsequent BG missions that I could reach and duly followed up converts I had counselled.

25.7.55 Sarah Jane Acton (our forth child) was born.

22.6.68 James Richard Benjamin Acton (our fifth child) arrived by design as did the others by God's grace.

Family Growth

As you can see, we have been blessed with five children who are happily married (one civil contract) and each couple has given us one or more grandchildren (eight to date). Some grandchildren have already married and given us six great grandchildren to date. Sadly Doreen and I have both lost our parents and siblings. But we keep in touch with the Acton, Bates and Mason families and occasionally get together. Way back we had lovely family holidays with the children.

Customs career.

I proceeded up the executive promotion ladder ,SEO,CEO and then Senior Inspector (SCEO equivalent). I stayed in London all this time despite being made the first Customs Staff Inspector; and later the departmental grade of Senior Inspector. Each time Head Office intervened after a while to keep me available in general personnel work. I think that God was behind this, as running the Brentwood Crusader Class and also keeping my family home and children's schooling stable, was a great privilege. Towards the end of my service I was rewarded with two invitations for Doreen and myself to Buckingham Palace Garden Parties. I retired at 60, December 1980. To my very great surprise I was awarded an OBE early the following year..

Chapter 32 - Retirement

During my 38 years service in Crusaders, I had very little spare time, as Doreen and Iwe were both active in Church and also ran a weekly Bible study home group. Doreen was very busy bringing up five children. I overdid my activities at one time and had to try and cut them down. Pressure eased a little as the children started University. Doreen was finally able to start her academic studies with the Open University, where she obtained a BA 2:1.

The adult children began getting degrees. Our first son Thomas had a specially distinctive career by achieving an Oxford Doctorate, with his rejected first thesis being published as "Gypsy Politics and Social Change". My former superior in Customs who became Sir Angus Fraser, later told me that he found Thomas' book 'Life-changing.' Greenwich University finally created a special Chair for Thomas and made him Professor of Romani Studies. He was made a FRSA and awarded a very well deserved OBE in 2009 for his work in education, particularly securing education for Gypsy and Traveller children in schools. As Emeritus Professor , Greenwich University, Senior Research Fellow IDRICS Bucks New

University and Visiting Professor Corvinus University, Budapest, Thomas is still very active at home and abroad, seeking to help these Romani minority groups of people. Thomas is married to Belinda, a nurse from Hong Kong. They have three children and six grandchildren to date.

Our other children and some of the grandchildren have also achieved a very great deal. First daughter Alice has an amazing number of qualifications ranging from B.Sc (Honours) in Physics and Mathematics and Post Graduate Certificate in Education (Sussex University) to supplementary courses on Teacher Effectiveness, Special Needs, British Council work, Information Technology for Special Needs Diploma (Keele University) - and this is not a complete list. She has done several teaching jobs ending as Deputy Principal of Burton Hill School (Malmesbury) for 8-19 years students with physical disabilities and learning difficulties. She does a lot of voluntary work and help at Malmesbury Abbey Church, 'Through the Roof' Charity, Food Bank ,etc. She is a talented creative artist in drawing, painting, patchwork, etc. She is well supported by Michael Langtree, her second husband. They have two daughters.

Second son Jonathan went to Reading University and gained a BA (Hons) in History and Archaeology and later, a MA qualification from Brookes in Historical and Art Historical Studies. He has had various jobs including some paid and unpaid voluntary work in Oxford Museums. He used to love going on various archaeological digs.. He helps at his local Baptist Church along with his wife Sam. She is from Malaysia and of Chinese extraction. She is a highly skilled Agency Nurse. They have one daughter Jennifer who is a Doctor of Opthalmology and mentioned below, where I refer to getting Macular Degeneration in my Nineties.

Second daughter Sarah tried various jobs and then qualified as a Psychiatric Nurse. She helps with Sunday School work at our local Brentwood Baptist Church. She is married to Paul Beniston, who retired from his Chartered Accountant job to undertake missionary trips to Calcutta with Sarah. The Indian climate upset Sarah's health so they settled back after a while in Doddinghurst. They have one son.

Third son James gained a 2;1 in Mathematics at Warwick University and then a M Phil in Statistics at Liverpool University. He is currently employed by HM Revenue and Customs as an Analyst. In the last three years he moved from a London flat to a chalet bungalow in the road behind ours, positioned so that the ends of our gardens adjoin. Thus he is able to keep an eye on my wife and self in our nineties. Also he is a very great help to us with our computer problems. His partner, Dr Elsa Damien, is French and a language expert. They are bringing up their lovely four year old son to be bi-lingual.

Piano teaching career (1982 to 2011)

Following my Civil Service retirement, I spent roughly a year on DIY improvements to the house and garden. My piano playing had necessarily been of a low-key nature in my working years. I had done very little teaching or performing. Here was a chance to begin to enjoy more exploration of the classics for myself, and begin modest home piano teaching to children and adults. To my delight I found teaching piano one to one delightful. I met some lovely children and adults and pupils shot up to 20+ a week. Grandson Timothy achieve grade eight at 15 and the three Taylor girls from Church achieved two grade eights and a grade seven. At one time I was running Junior and Senior workshops which were much enjoyed by me and my pupils. I also composed short pieces which I would print out dedicated specially for each pupil. I called them Whimsies. Timothy loved his personal Whimsy and memorised it at a very early stage. Later on I began giving home piano recitals of the classics in aid of the British Red Cross.

Chapter 33- Children's and Teenage Novels .

Shortly after taking over the Senior Leadership of the Brentwood Crusader Class from Mr Lindsay German, I encouraged senior sixth-formers to help lead opening sessions of the Sunday afternoon class. One such was David Ison who spoke well and introduced a novel feature, a short extract from the adventures of 'Super-Cru', a character he had invented - fiction but with a Christian bias. The children loved it and brought their friends, eager to hear the next instalment. Maybe a controversial item, but we made a clear distinction between Super-Cru and the solid Bible teaching and hymn and chorus singing which occupied 90% or more of the class time.

In five or six weeks David and his identical twin brother Keith, had to leave to go to University. What was I to do? After prayer I quickly invented another character, 'Jack Banks', a thirteen year old son of missionary parents. He is sent to England to a boarding school. He is shy and endures various trials until Christian friends and teachers lead him to make the great 'Discovery'. I had to write a new episode for each week and semi-memorise it, so as to keep my eyes on the boys. To my relief they kept on bringing their friends and the class grew from about 25 to 50+ boys every Sunday afternoon. We won the national Crusader recruiting shield for the year. Then I wrote 'Jack Banks on Trial', a sequel to the first Jack Banks story.

For my teenage piano students, I wrote 'Martin Ashworth Fourteen' using musical forms (particularly first movement sonata form) to guide the narrative, with an appendix to show how I had done this plus brief notes on musical form. I wrote a sequel 'Martin Ashworth Fourteen Plus in normal format. I also wrote two more junior novels 'Ben Bugden Thirteen' and 'The King's Son'. The latter is allegorical in nature and is set many hundred of years ago in a Middle Eastern country. It has a reference to God but no specific Christian slant which the other five novels have. I wrote it so that I could give it to foreign pupils (Indian, Saudi etc piano pupils) without giving offence.

I also hoped that it might be useful in showing the futility of wars based upon a history of distrust. between tribes.

I typed these stories and copied the pages at home. Then published them in a loose-leaf format with my own ISBN numbers. I also printed them in my 'pianist-storyteller.blogspot.com' blog. Later my youngest son James helped me get them into Kindle Ebooks and finally into glossy paperbacks by Create Space. They are available from Amazon where I have been given an Author's Page.

Doreen and I were privileged to be invited to David Ison's installation as Dean of St Paul's Cathedral on25th May 2012. At the very end of the long ceremony, David himself, as a good pastor, was at the door saying a word to the remaining few who were leaving. I had not seen him for thirty years, although we had kept in touch with Christmas letters. He recognised me with a start. After a few words, he said he was chuffed that his 'Super Cru' stories had led to my novel writing..

Chapter 34 - Current life

My piano teaching ended abruptly on 6th May 2011 after I had given a public two hours recital of classical music with a half-hour tea break at Valence House Museum. It was to celebrate the restoration of a 1828 grand piano and also became my 'Swan-song'.

Family, friends, my two brilliant Sri Lankan senior pupils and members of the public crowded the very narrow audience space. It was successful in that I was being asked if I could come again some time But my right eye had developed Macular Degeneration. I had to politely refuse. I was 90 and in a few days, my left eye also developed MD. I could no longer read small print or music. So I could not continue teaching the five or six pupils I still had. I was fortunate that both my eyes have settled into a dry age related MD condition, with only a very slow deteriorating   starting. Strangely we have a grand-daughter Jennifer, a Doctor of Opthalmology, who has been researching MD here and in America. She has given me some useful advice. So now I am writing these memoirs on an extra large computer screen, provided by my expert and tender-hearted son James. He also gave me a Kindle Reader.

Before I close I must apologise to the very many notable unmentioned. Christian leaders, family, friends, young people boys and girls who did so much for me. By rights they all should have had an individual mention in this account. I must confess that the strain of research and eye weakness at 94/95 plus laziness is my only excuse. Readers may be interested to know that Renown Pictures Ltd have issued a remastered DVD of the 1937 film "Talking Feet". Eldest son Thomas gave it to me two or three years ago. It was a huge surprise. I believe it is still available to buy. Also the Renown Film Club tell me that it is occasionally shown on their Talking Pictures TV Channel 81'

At 93 and 95 Doreen and I have been happily married for 68 years and rejoice in our large family and many friends. Above all we cherish the gracious love of our heavenly Father and Jesus, who revealed Himself to us as we have walked together on our own Emmaus Road, as prophesied in our wedding sermon by the Rev. John Pritchard.

John George Acton   March 2016

Still together – with Leila, sixth great-grandchild in 2014

(Photo taken by Alastair Roberts)

Printed in Great Britain
by Amazon